Dan Rice

Akitas

Everything about Purchase, Care,
Nutrition, Behavior, and Training

With 47 Color Photographs

Illustrations By Michele Earle-Bridges

BARRON'S

Dedication

This book is dedicated to my mentor, editor, and friend at Barron's, Mary Falcon. It couldn't have happened without the technical help of Lynn Snickles, a local Akita breeder, and I am indebted also to Sophia Kaluzniacki, D.V.M, for her contribution. The never-ending patience and proofreading by my wife, Marilyn, was invaluable, as always.

© Copyright 1997 by Barron's Educational Series, Inc.

All inquiries should be addressed to:
Barron's Educational Series, Inc.
250 Wireless Boulevard
Hauppauge, NY 11788

International Standard Book No. 0-7641-0075-0

Library of Congress Catalog Card No. 97-1064

Library of Congress Cataloging-in-Publication Data
Rice, Dan, 1933–
    Akitas : everything about purchase, care,
  nutrition, breeding, behavior, and training / Dan
  Rice ; illustrations by Michele Earle-Bridges.
       p.   cm.—(A complete pet owner's manual)
    Includes bibliographical references (p.) and
index.
    ISBN 0-7641-0075-0
    1. Akita dogs. I. Title. II. Series.
  SF429.A65R53 1997
  636.73—dc21   97-1064
                                                   CIP

Printed in Hong Kong

9876

About the Author

Dan Rice is a veterinarian from Colorado, presently pursuing a life-long avocation in writing. This is his fourth book for Barron's. Now retired in sunny Arizona, some of his greatest memories are of the hundreds of northern dogs—including Akitas—that dominated his practice in the cold and snowy Rocky Mountains.

Photo Credits

Barbara Augello: pages 45, 76, 89 left; Paulette Braun: pages 53, 69, 88, 92 bottom; Kent and Donna Dannen: inside back cover; pages 8 bottom, 20, 25, 57, 81; Susan Green: front cover, pages 8 top, 9, 13, 16, 44 top right, 44 top left, 72; Larry Johnson: pages 29, 41; Sophia Kaluzniacki: pages 36, 84; Zig Leszczynski: pages 33, 40 top, 44 bottom left, 68, 77 top and bottom; Bob Schwartz: back cover, page 32 bottom; Lynn Snickles: page 24; Judith Strom: pages 48, 52, 92 top; Toni Tucker: pages 17, 49, 60, 93; Siobhan Valentine: page 73; Wim van Vugt: pages 4, 5, 32 top, 40 bottom, 44 bottom right, 56, 85, 89 right.

Important Note

This pet owner's guide tells the reader how to buy and care for an Akita dog. The author and the publisher consider it important to point out that the advice given in the book is meant primarily for normally developed puppies from a good breeder—that is, dogs of excellent physical health and good character.

Anyone who adopts a fully grown dog should be aware that the animal has already formed its basic impressions of human beings. The new owner should watch the animal carefully, including its behavior toward humans, and should meet the previous owner. If the dog comes from a shelter, it may be possible to get some information on the dog's background and peculiarities there. There are dogs that, as a result of bad experiences with humans, behave in an unnatural manner or may even bite. Only people that have experience with dogs should take in such animals.

Caution is further advised in the association of children with dogs, in meeting with other dogs, and in exercising the dog without a leash.

Even well-behaved and carefully supervised dogs sometimes do damage to someone else's property or cause accidents. It is therefore in the owner's interest to be adequately insured against such eventualities, and we strongly urge all dog owners to purchase a liability policy that covers their dog.

Contents

Introduction 6
Origin of the Canine Species 6
Human Influence 6
Selective Breeding 7
Domestication 7
Human Stewardship 8
Akita History 10

Akita Characteristics 12
The Akita's Unique Features 12
Show Standards 13
The AKC Standard for the Akita 14
The Akita's Personality 16
Historical Importance and Uses
  of Akitas 18
The Akita's Value as a Pet 19

Choosing Your Akita 21
Timing 21
What to Look For 21
Quality 22
Why an Akita? 25
Choosing a Young Puppy 26
Obtaining an Older Dog 27
Which Sex to Choose 28
Sources 29
Personality 30
Health Status 31
Veterinarians 33
Breeder's Guarantees 34
Registration 35

Bringing Your Akita Home 36
A Puppy in the House 36
A Puppy in the Yard 36
HOW-TO: Puppy-Proofing Your
  Home 38
Bonding with Your Akita 40
Keeping Your Akita Healthy 41
Feeding Your Akita 41
Providing a Kennel and Run 42
Traveling by Car with Your Akita 43

Training Your Akita 45
The Importance of Obedience
  Training 45
Crate Training 46
Housebreaking 46
Introducing the Collar and
  Leash 47
Leash Training 48
Command Clarity 49
Basic Commands 49

Caring for Your Akita 53
Teeth and Their Care 53
Ear Care 54
Calluses 54
Boarding 54
Veterinary Care 55
Spaying 55
Castration 57
HOW-TO: Grooming
  Your Akita 58

Akita Activities 60
Exercise 60
Canine Good Citizen Tests 61
Weight Pulling, Skijoring, and
  Sledding 61
Agility 62
Dog Showing 63
HOW-TO: Entertaining
  Your Akita 64

Nutrition 66
Components of a Good Diet 66
Commercial Dog Foods 66
Types of Foods 68
Supplements 68
Homemade Diets, Snacks,
  and Treats 69
Frequency of Feeding 69

Breeding Your Akita 70
Pre-Breeding Evaluation 70
Phases of the Estrous Cycle 71
Pregnancy 71
Nesting 72
Whelping 72
When to Call for Help 74
Post-Whelping Problems 74

Puppy Care 75
Feeding the Lactating Female 75
Monitoring the Puppies 75
Dewclaw Amputation 77

Weaning 77
Socialization 78
Prospective Buyers 78
Physical Exam and Vaccinations 78
Care of the Dam's Coat 79

Akita Health Care 80
When to Retire a Brood Bitch 80
Diseases Prevented by Vaccinations 80
Other Common Diseases and
  Health Problems 82
Euthanasia 88

**Registration, Pedigrees, and
  Titles 90**
Litter Registration 90
Pedigrees 90
Titles 91

Useful Literature and Addresses 94

Index 95

There's no guarantee that a puppy will grow up to be breed or show quality, so buy it for love.

Introduction

Origin of the Canine Species

The exact origin of *Canis familiaris* will likely remain obscure in spite of the investigations of scores of learned researchers. Many strange and sometimes conflicting theories have been advanced regarding the prehistoric ancestors of modern domestic canines. Some contemporary authorities would have us believe that all dog breeds are descendants of the wolf. Certainly there are various sizes and colors of wolves, with those of the Northern Hemisphere being larger than those of the southern climates. Smaller races also are indigenous to India and China.

Some references place the domestic dog in partnership with humans during the Stone Age, some 50,000 years ago. Those reports are based on archeological evidence, including partial skeletons and miscellaneous bones or bone fragments of animals resembling those of modern dogs. Current studies place the dog in human company a short 14,000 years ago, from the end of the Ice Age.

When we step closer to the present time, it is easier to speculate about our pooch's family tree. The family Canidae, including domestic dogs and their feral cousins the foxes, jackals, coyotes, wolves, and others, have many common characteristics. Their teeth are adapted to seizing and tearing, and they have acute olfactory (smelling) and auditory (hearing) senses. They are instinctively social animals that form packs or family groups.

Canines' psychological development relates to their association with others in the pack or family group, and they follow the guidance of dominant leaders. They maintain central headquarters, regions, or dens that they defend, and they routinely deposit scent trails to stake out their claim to those areas. Regardless of their prehistoric ancestors, companion dogs have many similarities to those wild animals.

If the reader is interested in perusing the many dog-origin theories, there are numerous authoritative encyclopedic articles and books in the library. Pick the theory you like best, and read to your heart's content. After digesting the volumes of historical information, one question will remain with you: Do my Akita and your Chihuahua have a common ancestry with Grandpa's bulldog and Aunt Hilda's Pekingese? The evidence points toward an affirmative answer.

Human Influence

One thing is certain: Humans and their best friends, dogs, have enjoyed a long and fruitful relationship, one that predates written history. That mutually beneficial companionship is depicted in petroglyphs that decorate the walls of cavemen's homes. It is confirmed by prominent paintings and sculptures of dogs that were found among relics of ancient civilizations.

Artifacts and petroglyphs point to the probability of domestic dogs living in association with virtually every aboriginal Indian tribe in North America, long before European visitors came to the continent. Of approximately 20 breeds or types believed to have been native to North America, only Eskimo dogs and the Mexican hairless currently exist in their original shape and form.

Ancient tombs of Japanese people of the eleventh and twelfth centuries were frequently decorated with the likenesses of Akitas. The prick ears and curled tail are preserved as unmistakable evidence of Akita-like dogs that were companions of people of that period and culture.

Selective Breeding

Genetic engineering, by means of gene splicing and chromosome manipulations, may produce changes in a single generation. Those high-tech laboratory processes haven't been used to produce new breeds or varieties within a breed (yet). In the dog, laboratory genetic engineering is unnecessary if we have a little patience. Canines come equipped with an easily manipulated genetic structure, one that allows conformation changes to be altered quickly by selective breeding. Considering that dogs can raise a litter every year, and are capable of reproducing before one year of age, a new generation can easily be spawned annually.

Dogs of the same genotype (genetic properties) have the capacity to vary in phenotype (visible and behavioral properties). Phenotype changes are produced naturally by the interaction of genotype and the environment. By choosing dogs that display certain desirable traits, and by using those dogs in a breeding scheme, many canine physical characteristics can be molded and changed rather easily. That is known as selective breeding techniques.

Phenotype Malleability

Perhaps you wish to put more curl in your Akitas' tails. By careful selection of a few dogs that possess tightly curled tails, a gene pool is quickly established that possesses that phenotype. In the first generation of puppies

produced from those selected parents, those with the sought-after curly tail are mated. Within a few generations, the curly tail should be routinely obtained in a majority of puppies produced. The characteristic is indelibly and quickly stamped on the progeny.

This simplified, hypothetical example is intended to illustrate the concept of phenotype malleability. There are many pitfalls to dog breeding based on selection for a single physical characteristic, and the example is not meant to advocate such activity; it is only intended to promote the idea of the plasticity of canine physical characteristics. Careful selective breeding may or may not be the answer to the origin of the hundreds of dog breeds of so many sizes and shapes presently populating the earth. It is certainly the method used to produce minor phenotypic changes such as the behavior, various coat types, and color patterns seen within breeds such as the Akita.

Domestication

How did dog and human form their partnership? That's another provocative question, the answer for which is buried in antiquity. It is logical to assume that "dogs" first existed apart from humans. They were probably wild carnivores, animals that survived by hunting, killing, and eating their prey. *Canis familiaris'* wild cousins give us modern, visible evidence of their ancestor's probable habits and lifestyles.

Wolves are a good example. They are governed by a pack leader, hunt together, share the spoils, and sometimes they care for each others' offspring. That dogs follow a leader, or alpha member, of their pack gives us a likely reason for their early domestication by humans. A human was substituted for the alpha dog, and assumed dominance and leadership in the pack. Dogs probably joined human company seeking an easily available source of

A romp in the woods with your Akita.

food and shelter. Since they are masters of body language, they are able to communicate readily with human beings. Those that refused to submit to human domination were eliminated;

A fine specimen of the Akita breed.

they may have been rejected from society, or they provided meat for the stew pot and pelts for clothing. By that primitive, unplanned selection, they became helpmates to the people who kept them.

When humans recognized the animals' hunting expertise and guarding ability, and their acceptance of subservient roles in society, they began to claim them as companions and junior partners, and the dogs quickly earned the title of "man's best friend."

Throughout history, dogs have served humankind in hundreds of roles. It is only natural that humans should select and breed dogs of the size, color, and temperament that please them or best fill their particular needs; thus, we now have hundreds of different dog breeds from which to choose. Some have been specialized in function to scent out and retrieve upland birds; others have been selected by size and strength to hunt bears, boars, and other big game. There are those that have the brawn to challenge other dogs in fights, and still others that have the stamina to carry a pack or pull a cart. In some primitive societies, dogs are still raised for their meat. Akita heritage includes all these qualities. Their uses and purposes are nearly endless.

Human Stewardship

The availability of great variety and selection isn't all good news. A natural side effect of choice is to lose the sense of value of a living pet or to reject one animal in favor of another. This has led to the destruction of millions of wonderful canine pets that people obtained with the best intentions, only to discover later that the animal selected didn't fit into their household.

Unfortunately, representatives of our Akita breed are also seen in this scenario. Although there are no statistics to show how many Akitas wind up in dog

The elegant beauty of an Akita.

pounds every year, abandoned and destroyed, the number must be significant. Too often, the adorable face of an Akita puppy leads a family to purchase the dog but a year later, with no socialization and little training, the dog becomes a liability to the owner and the neighborhood and winds up in the hands of the dog warden.

Rejected American pets now number in the hundreds of thousands. They occupy dog pounds and animal shelters across the country. When those facilities can no longer house them, they are euthanized in enormous numbers.

Canine overpopulation can only be reduced by responsible dog owners and breeders. That includes all of us who obtain dogs and don't have them sexually neutered before they reach reproductive age. We must accept our human role of pet stewardship as a primary consideration when we decide to obtain a dog. That is critically important, whether shopping for an expensive purebred, show-quality Akita, or when looking for a free, mixed-breed pup for a child's pet.

Professional or incidental Akita breeders should employ a neutering

9

policy for all pets sold; contracts can be used to ensure that the policy is followed. All prospective dog breeders should be aware that only the best examples of their chosen breed should be used in a breeding program. Dog overpopulation is exacerbated by irresponsible purebred breeders that assume all registered dogs are breeding quality.

Akita History

The Akita breed is steeped in history. Early historical accounts include its flesh as a menu item, and its skin was valued for making warm garments. It served as a working dog, a fighter, and a hunter; some have been used in the fishing industry.

Details of the Akita's history have been obscured by centuries of isolation on the remote Japanese island of Honshu, and sometimes it has been muddied by language and translation problems. Typical Akita-like dogs, with tightly curled tails and erect ears, were evident as early as 1150 A.D.

The Akita was known as *Matagiinu*, the esteemed hunter, by Japanese royalty. At one time, ownership of an Akita was limited to the rulers of Japan, who decked them out with special collars to designate the rank of the owner. They were treated to all the niceties, and the best diet that Japanese royalty had to offer.

During the next several hundred years, Akitas' popularity rose and fell with the Japanese dynasties, depending on the habits and desires of the ruling classes. Then, in the time of Emperor Taisho, around the turn of the twentieth century, the dog fancy became popular. Following the styles of Great Britain, France, and Spain, dogs became a status symbol among the populace and royalty alike. The European influence revived the interest in Akitas, and once again they gained importance in Japan.

The Akita Stud Book

Although Akita-type dogs were raised in many Japanese regions, the large northern strains produced in the mountainous Akita Prefecture were undoubtedly the most influential ancestors of today's Akita. In 1927 the Akita Inu Hozankai society was given the task of recording and maintaining a stud book that documented the parents of every litter produced in Japan. It persists today and helps to preserve the purity of the breed.

Odate Dogs

Originally known as Odate dogs, Akitas were recognized in 1931 as a national monument—a Japanese treasure—and were officially named as a pure breed. That action was taken by the mayor of Odate, the capitol of the Akita Prefecture, the northernmost province of the Japanese Island of Honshu. Japanese dogs are customarily named for the region in which they prevailed, and their original name was Akita Inu (Akita dog). They were the largest of seven Japanese breeds established in 1931. Akitas' pedigree documentation has been carefully maintained at Odate since that time.

World War II and After

Akita numbers dwindled in their native Japan during World War II when they were in demand for food and pelts. Others were destroyed to conserve food that might be used for human consumption. Although they neared extinction, representatives of the breed somehow survived, and they began to flourish again in the post-war years of the late 1940s and early 1950s. Akita breeding during that period resulted in the production of two bloodlines, the descendants of which have emigrated to virtually the entire world.

American and allied servicemen are probably responsible for the early popularity of Akitas in the United States and other Western countries. Many American soldiers were so enamored by the sturdiness, loyalty, and beauty of the breed that they acquired the dogs and brought them home. During the post-war years of 1945 to 1955 a great number of Akitas were imported into the United States, England, and Canada.

AKC Acceptance

By 1955 a breed club was established in the United States, and the American Kennel Club (AKC) accepted Akitas for exhibition in their miscellaneous classes. In 1972 they were given individual breed showing status by the AKC. The Akita of the Western world has, by most accounts, retained the important Japanese Akita characteristics (see breed standard, page 14).

Some Well-Known Akitas

No discussion of Akita history is complete without mention of two animals. Hachi-Ko was an Akita given to a Tokyo professor in 1924. The professor rode a commuter train to and from his suburban home daily, and Hachi-Ko accompanied him to the station in the morning and returned to the station to meet him each evening. When Professor Ueno died from a stroke, Hachi-Ko continued to make his daily trips to the train station at the exact hours previously established, and after waiting for the train, and his master, he walked home alone. Although the dog was only about 18 months old when the professor succumbed to the stroke, Hachi-Ko continued walking to the station every evening until his own death, nearly ten years later. A bronze statue of Hachi-Ko stands at Toyko's Shibuya Station today, and a ceremony attracts hundreds of dog fanciers to the station to honor Hachi-Ko each year.

United States humanitarian Helen Keller met and fell in love with Akitas during a Japanese speaking tour in 1937. She was presented with a puppy, Kamikaze-Go, that she brought home to New York, but unfortunately it died before one year of age. In 1939 another Akita, Kanzan-Go, was given to her and it lived as her companion until its death in 1945.

Akita Characteristics

Akitas come in a variety of eye-catching colors and patterns. Any color and color combination is seen on them, including white, brindle, and pinto, or spotted. Their markings are brilliant and clear, and never smudged. The pinto Akita probably has the most outstanding appearance, with a white ground color and large, evenly spaced patches of dark color over the body.

Their conformation is in many ways similar to the sled dogs of Alaska and Siberia; they were developed under similar conditions, in another frigid part of the world. Certainly their body type is that of a northern working dog, strong and muscular.

As in all purebred dog husbandry, selective breeding has brought about changes in Akitas' physical characteristics from those of the original Japanese animals. They are larger, more massive animals today than they were in the twelfth century. Because of the depletion of the breeding stock pool during World War II, Akitas of today may be traced to a small number of progenitors. Those bred and exhibited in America and Great Britain tend to reflect the post-war development of the breed in the United States.

Akitas bred in Japan are usually smaller in stature, with lighter bone structure than their Western counterparts. Japanese-bred dogs may also sport smaller ears, an outstanding coat quality, and sharp, distinct coat patterns. In Japanese shows, the Akitas are "faced off," encouraging them to show aggressiveness. The Japanese seem to cultivate and appreciate this trait in their dogs, and breed toward it.

The Akita's Unique Features

It would be a serious judgment error to try to discuss all the characteristics that set Akitas apart from the rest of the canine species but an error of equal magnitude would be to neglect to mention a few of those features.

Size: The males stand 26 to 28 inches (66 to 71 cm) at the withers; females are 24 to 26 inches (61 to 66 cm). Their weights, although not mentioned in the standard, average 95 to 110 pounds (43 to 50 kg) for males and 75 to 90 pounds (34 to 41 kg) for females. Their thick, short, arched

An Akita's bone structure.

12

necks, dense coats, and bulky bodies give them the appearance of much larger animals. Fanciers have stated that Akitas are at the lower end of the large breeds, not at the upper end of middle-sized breeds. When seen briefly and alone, the visual image retained is that of much larger dogs.

Color: One particularly attractive Akita feature is the wide variety of body colors found in the breed. Virtually all colors are acceptable from white to black, including red, silver, fawn, brindle, and pinto. The attractive pinto color patterns are said to be attributable primarily to a post-war dog named Goromaru-Go. He sported flashy red and white pinto colors that were indelibly stamped on his progeny. The breed standards specify that Akita colors should be sharp and distinct with clear-cut markings that aren't smudged or masked.

Head: Akita heads also exhibit various colors and patterns. Some dogs have solid colored heads; others sport dazzling, impressive white markings. Masks and blazes are often seen, and if equilaterally balanced, they are acceptable and greatly admired. Once you have adjusted to the flashy colors and markings of the dogs, your attention is immediately drawn to their broad, triangular heads.

Face: Akitas' faces are truly remarkable. Their expressions are dominated by wide-set small ears that tip forward, giving them an alert or curious appearance, even when resting. Those appendages seem to lead your gaze next to their dark brown, smallish, almond shaped, oriental eyes.

Tail: Although there is a lot of dog between the head and tail, your next point of concentration might be the Akita's tail. It is large and full, set high, and carried over the back or against the flank in a three-quarter, full, or double curl, always dipping to or below the level of the back. It has coarse, straight

A beautiful pinto Akita.

hair, with no plume, and is rarely stationary. Akita tails that aren't curled or that are carried away from their backs are considered serious faults.

Coat: Akita coats, like those of other northern dogs, are double, with coarse, dense, plush guard hair, and soft, dense undercoats. The luxurious coat quality can't be overlooked or understated. It shows no signs of feathering on the legs, and adds to the bulky, sturdy appearance of the entire body (see standard, page 15).

Show Standards

The Akita Club of America was formed in 1956, and the breed was admitted to registration in the AKC in 1972. In terms of U.S. registry, the breed is somewhat new, although its history is traced back hundreds of years in Japan. Akitas were admitted to regular AKC show classification in the Working Group in April, 1973. Worldwide, Akitas are bred to several standards, depending on the country

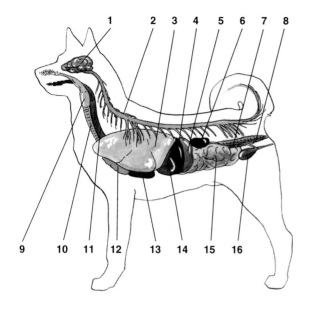

1. Brain
2. Spinal cord
3. Lungs
4. Stomach
5. Spleen
6. Kidney
7. Ureter
8. Descending colon
9. Larynx
10. Trachea
11. Esophagus
12. Thymus
13. Heart
14. Liver
15. Jejunum
16. Bladder

Internal organs.

where they are produced and shown. Before you buy a dog, regardless of age or color, you should study the breed standard and attend shows and matches to see how the animals are professionally judged and evaluated. Take time to talk to breeders, and try to understand why a judge placed one dog above another in a class. In doing so, you will familiarize yourself with the most important characteristics of the breed.

The American Kennel Club (AKC) breed standards are available upon request from the AKC. Study the standard (below) and memorize the important distinguishing characteristics listed.

You will find that every category of the Akita conformation standard belabors adjectives such as: *large, heavy, broad, firm, wide, deep, strong, thick, muscular,* and *hard.* Their temperaments are variously described as *courageous, dominant, dignified, vigorous,* and *resilient.* Those terms paint a picture of a powerful working animal, one that is aloof and sure of itself.

The AKC Standard for the Akita

The following specifications are listed in the AKC breed standard:

General Appearance

The Akita is large, powerful, alert, with much substance and heavy bone. Its broad head forms a blunt triangle, with a deep muzzle, small eyes, and erect ears that are carried forward in line with back of the neck. The large, curled tail, balancing the broad head, is characteristic of the breed.

The Head and Neck

Head: the head is massive but in balance with the body and free of wrinkles when the dog is at ease. The skull is flat between the ears and broad. The jaws are square and powerful with a minimal dewlap. The head forms a blunt triangle when it is viewed from above. Fault: a narrow head.

Muzzle: The muzzle is broad and full, and the distance from the nose to the stop as compared to the distance from the stop to the occiput is as 2 is to 3. The stop is well defined, but not too abrupt. A shallow furrow extends well up the forehead.

Nose: The nose is broad and black. Liver color is permitted on white Akitas but black is always preferred. Disqualifications: a butterfly nose or total lack of pigmentation on the nose.

Ears: The ears are strongly erect and small in relation to rest of head. If an ear is folded forward for measuring length, the tip will touch the upper eye rim. The ears are triangular, slightly rounded at the tip, wide at the base, set wide on the head, but not too low. They are carried slightly forward over the eyes, in line with the back of the neck. Disqualification: drop or broken ears.

Eyes: The eyes are dark brown, small, deep-set, and triangular in shape. The rims of the eyes are black and tight.

Lips and tongue: The lips are black and not pendulous. The tongue is pink.

Teeth: The teeth are strong. A scissors bite is preferred, but a level bite is acceptable. Disqualifications: a noticeably undershot or overshot jaw.

Neck: The neck is thick, muscular, and comparatively short. It widens gradually toward the shoulders. It has a pronounced crest that blends in with the base of the skull.

The Body and Tail

Body: The body is longer than high, the chest is wide and deep, and the depth of the chest is one-half the height of the dog at the shoulder. The ribs are well sprung, and the brisket is well developed. The Akita has a level back with a firmly muscled loin and moderate tuck-up (flank). The skin is pliant but not loose. Serious faults: light bone structure or a rangy body.

Tail: The tail is large, full, set high, and carried over the back or against the flank in a three-quarter, full, or double curl. The tail should always dip to or below the level of the back. On a three-quarter curl, the tip should drop well down the flank. The root of the tail is large and strong, and the tail bone reaches the hock when it is let down. The tail hair is coarse, straight, and full, with no appearance of a plume. Disqualifications: a sickle tail or an uncurled tail.

Forequarters and hindquarters: In the forequarters, the shoulders are strong and powerful with a moderate layback. The forelegs are heavy boned and straight when viewed from the front. The angle of the pastern is 15 degrees forward from the vertical. Faults: elbows that turn in or out or loose shoulders.

The width and muscular development of the hindquarters are comparable to that of the forequarters. The upper thighs are well developed and the stiffles are moderately bent. The hocks are well let down, and turn neither in nor out.

The dewclaws on the front legs are generally not removed, but they are usually removed from the hind legs. The Akita has cat feet that are well knuckled up, with thick pads, and they point straight ahead.

The Coat

Akitas have double coats; the undercoat is thick, soft, dense, and shorter than the outer coat. The outer coat is straight, harsh, and stands somewhat off the body. The hair on the head, legs, and ears is short. The length of the hair at the withers and rump is approximately two inches long, which is slightly longer than the hair on the rest of the body except the tail, where the coat is longest and most profuse. Fault: any indication of ruff or feathering.

Color: Any color is allowed, including white, brindle, or pinto. The colors are brilliant and clear and the markings are well balanced, with or without a mask or blaze. White Akitas have no mask. The pinto has a white background with large, evenly placed patches covering the head and more that one-third of the body. The undercoat may be a different color from the outer coat.

Gait and Size

Gait: The Akita moves with brisk and powerful strides of moderate length. The back remains strong, firm, and level. The rear legs move in line with the front legs.

Size: Males should measure 26 to 28 inches (66–71 cm) at the withers and bitches 24 to 26 inches (61–66 cm). Disqualifications: dogs that stand

A pair of Akitas at play.

under 25 inches (63 cm) or bitches that measure under 23 inches (58 cm).

Temperament

The Akita should be alert and responsive, dignified and courageous. It is characteristically aggressive toward other dogs.

The Akita's Personality

Some irresponsible breeders will tell you that the Akita's temperament is dependent on its environment as a puppy. That is only partially correct. The disposition of an Akita is the product of its early home life, handling, socialization, and *heredity*.

Dog-Aggressive

Akitas are generally considered dog-aggressive. They are usually outgoing, fun-loving, and friendly toward other pets they have known since puppyhood, although this is not always the case. They are not always trustworthy around dogs with which they are raised, and should not be allowed off leash when other dogs are in the vicinity. Adults should always be walked with a chain choke collar and short, stout leash, since control must be exercised when strange dogs are encountered. They are strong willed, and must receive early socialization and regular training to control their aggressiveness. They are fierce and dominating when challenged by other dogs, and their curious, mischievous natures sometimes lead to such challenges. Few if any timid or reclusive Akitas are to be found.

People-Aggressive

Akitas are also considered by most breeders to be people-aggressive if not properly socialized while still puppies. To reduce this human-aggressive trait, they should be taken for walks in the park and put in contact with humans at every opportunity. Socialization is most effective when the dogs are young. As soon as your pup has had its vaccinations, teach it people manners while its leash training is underway. An Akita isn't apt to attack human beings who are minding their own business, but it should be introduced to other humans, and the earlier the better.

Some Akitas are nonaggressive until a year or more of age, when they change and become notably dominant. To their families, they are always intelligent, lovable, and trainable, yet stubborn—they definitely have a mind of their own. After a year of age, most Akitas will become more possessive and defensive of their families and property. At maturity, they are usually aggressive toward other animals, and sometimes toward strange people.

A personal acquaintance of mine, who is an Akita breeder, tells a story about a plumber who came to the house to fix a drain. The plumber went to work under the sink after he was introduced to one of the family's Akitas who happened to be in the house at the time. The family was busy in another part of the house. The dog quietly took each tool in the plumber's bag, carried it to the front door, and when everything was thus arranged, he returned and gently but firmly took the plumber's pants leg and escorted him to the front door!

Everyone needs hugs.

General Qualities

That story isn't meant to imply that all Akitas have such cleverness and intelligence. Certainly they can't be lumped into a common disposition mold, but there are some generalities that apply. Typically, Akitas are bright, but reserved. They are happy dogs in their own bailiwick, but they are always possessive. Adults shouldn't be silly or disposed to foolishness; timidity is a personality fault. An Akita should not be overtly aggressive.

Several authors describe the most desirable Akita temperament as *courageous* or *dignified*. Those terms, if a bit esoteric, are fine descriptions. Unfortunately, they are adjectives that

are difficult to apply to animals without considerable personal interaction with those creatures.

Akitas are affectionate creatures. They show no signs of aggression toward humans who are minding their own business, but they have a family loyalty defensive trait that is quickly shown to strangers who approach their homes. They are effective watch dogs, without any training or encouragement.

Defensive Qualities

Akitas seem to have innate, defensive qualities of their own. The breeder who told the plumber story above relates another story about her dog's natural protective instincts. When walking the dog, she found her Akita pushing her off the sidewalk when strangers were encountered on the street. Her dog, walking at heel on her left side, was positioned between his mistress and the rest of the world. When they met someone on the sidewalk, he gradually exerted pressure on her left knee, pushing her to one side, assuring that a wide berth was established between the stranger and his mistress.

Akita owners and breeders seem to agree that you should always carefully introduce your Akita to your friends, making it plain that those people's presence in your home is agreeable with you. The perceptive Akita will identify those persons who are not your friends without any help or training.

Akitas and Children

Akitas are not known to have short tempers with their family's children; they are tolerant and usually prefer to retreat when the play becomes tiresome, rather than snap at youngsters. They have historically been associated with guarding children, and commonly show great affection for boys and girls with whom they are raised. Their hunting instincts, stamina, and playful dispositions make them wonderful playmates for children of all ages.

However, when strange children or adults enter the picture, the Akita may be more realistically depicted as a guard dog, and should be taken to the kennel or put out in the yard. Shedding its role of playmate and companion, the family Akita becomes defensive of the family and home. The pet that loves your children and would go to great lengths to protect them, might see any stranger, regardless of age, as an interloper to be dealt with. A household filled with the confusion of children or adults passing in and out at random, makes a poor environment for an Akita.

Another story comes to mind. An Akita owner's five boys were wrestling on the floor when another ten-year-old boy from across the street decided to

join in the fun. When he tried to get into the pile of wrestling youngsters, the Akita barked at him, showed his teeth, and escorted him from the property. He didn't touch the child, and was quite content to "herd" the boy from the premises. He then returned to "his" boys and continued his vigil. Not all Akitas would be that polite, and to prevent problems in a similar situation, it would be best to physically separate the dog from the roughhousing.

Historical Importance and Uses of Akitas

Early development of Akitas blended the stubbornness and strong wills of fighting dogs with the scenting ability of sporting dogs. They were used to trail stags, bears, and other game, yet some of the earliest reports of Akitas relate to their roles in pit fighting. Although another Japanese breed (the Tosa, or Japanese mastiff) is better known for its fighting ability, the Akita's prowess in a dogfight is awesome.

That instinct hasn't been fully erased from their memories, as is evidenced by their contemporary never-quit attitude, their natural dominance over other dogs, and their winning ability in canine conflict. Housing two adult male Akitas together is risky business at best; it is never advisable. A male and female, or two females that were spayed before six months of age, may live together in harmony, but two males or two intact females will inevitably fight. Once a brawl has ensued, it is unlikely that peace and harmony will be found in the future.

Hunting: Akitas have been known to "nose out" game, and although never having made their mark in America as pointers or setters, in Japan they were used to locate and flush ground birds. History has it that they were accomplished soft-mouthed upland retrievers. They are large enough to bring down prey several times their weight and size, and were used to hunt deer and boar. Hunting bears was a challenge successfully met with a bow and arrow and a brace of aggressive and fearless Akitas that would keep the bear at bay until killed.

Water retrieving: Akitas are reported to flunk the test for water retrievers because of the character of their double coats that tend to absorb water. Their swimming abilities can't compare to the specialized hunting breeds of today, including spaniels, Labradors, Chesapeakes, and other proven water dogs. In spite of that limitation, there are reports of Akitas that were trained by fishermen to herd fish into their nets by swimming around them. An enviable feat, when you consider the quality and abundance of their coats.

Herding: Akitas were apparently used as herding dogs in the seventeenth century in the mountainous, northern regions of Honshu. That cold, snowy, northwest Sea of Japan environment no doubt exerted strong influence on the dogs' robust stamina, solid bone structure, and dense coats. Like other northern dogs of today, they retain much of the toughness of the environment of their origin.

Sledding: Akitas have proven themselves in weight-pulling contests on the ice, and those same dogs seem to be in their element when hitched to a sled. On the other hand, it is rare indeed to find Akitas that are used in sled teams together with malamutes and huskies. The reason is probably associated with the Akita propensity to dominate all other dogs in its society.

They are frequently photographed carrying back packs, and sometimes are shown harnessed to carts. There are reports of Akitas in police work, but that doesn't seem to be a suitable vocation for them, due to their natural aggressiveness.

Guard dog: Akitas are strong-willed animals that seem to have a wired-in protective instinct that isn't likely to be suppressed. All dogs have the ability to read human situations, probably through the detection and evaluation of certain pheromones (a type of scent given off by humans and perceived by the dog), originating from their owners, and perhaps from other dogs. They can sense fear or challenge when confronted by strange humans or dogs, even if no threatening gestures or sounds are made. A dominant Akita isn't apt to back down from anyone or anything.

The solid, tough, determined Akita is therefore an excellent guard dog without any special training whatsoever. Little or no encouragement is needed to whet its instinctive interest in protecting its home and family. Its strength, loyalty, and agility make it a formidable living security system in your home. Though it is a peace-loving pet, it will meet any challenge it perceives.

Warning: *To invest in guard training is a serious mistake, one that might convert a fine family companion into a monster.*

Some Akita breeders support this statement to the degree that they won't sell a puppy to anyone who intends to put it to work as a guard dog. Akitas overtrain easily, and take their training to heart, which ruins them as companion dogs and family pets. Akitas that have received guard training rarely make satisfactory pets!

The Akita's Value as a Pet

That brings us to the use most Akitas enjoy today. They make wonderful, winsome pets. Given a loving home and a caring family to look after, Akitas' value as pets and companions is second to none. Like all good pets, they respond to affection, kindness, and gentleness, and have the following admirable characteristics:

Akitas are natural guard dogs.

• They are quiet, unobtrusive, somewhat lazy dogs that enjoy human companionship.
• They are reported to fit well into an apartment (with regular exercise) and are quite at home in a fenced yard.
• They are playful with the children of the family, obedient (if a bit stubborn), and quite trainable.

An adult Akita is sometimes available for adoption. It may be a beautiful dog, but you should be very wary. Learn all you can about the dog before you decide to take it into your home. If it has had guard training, it's not the dog for you. Based on the opinions of breeders I have interviewed, there are few adult Akitas that have been rescued from pounds and other similar situations, where nothing is known about their background that can ever be trusted in a home with children.

Choosing Your Akita

Timing

A poor time to shop for pets is near the holidays, or shortly before you leave on vacation. Try to choose a convenient season, one that will allow you to devote a significant amount of "quality" time with the new family member. Select a period when you have few visitors, and when the family routine is quiet and stable. Don't introduce a new puppy into confusion and chaos. Adjustment to a new environment is a challenge for an Akita puppy, even under the best circumstances.

Reconsider any thoughts you might have about buying an Akita as a gift for anyone, unless that person is totally in accord with the idea, and then only if the timing is perfect. Don't impulsively purchase an Akita for a friend or family member. New pets must be discussed at length, and new owners must be physically, financially, and emotionally ready and willing to take on the responsibility of Akita ownership.

What to Look For

Because it is difficult to look at a two- or three-month-old puppy and visualize it as an adult, it is important to see its parents and, if possible, their adult offspring from previous litters. When you first see a litter of seven or eight week old cuddly little Akita puppies, you will appreciate the difficulty of comparing them to the 100-pound (45 kg) adults you have seen winning the purple and blue show ribbons. Be aware of the following:

• Puppies' small ears are folded down until about 9 to 14 weeks of age, and if they aren't up by 16 weeks of age, taping is required.
• Their tails begin to curl by the fourth week, and by eight weeks the typical Akita tail should be apparent. If a pup's tail isn't well curled by three to four months of age, it will probably remain uncurled throughout the animal's life. Although ears that don't spontaneously stand may be taped and trained, an uncurled tail is a fault that can't be corrected.
• The broad flat Akita forehead isn't terribly apparent in young puppies. Although the head type is usually discernible by a year of age, it continues to broaden for the next two to five years.
• The Akita usually gains its maximum height by 18 months or two years, then adds bulk until about five years.
• The Akita bite is a feature that is usually obvious in young pups. You should always check for the required scissors bite, with the upper incisors positioned just in front of and touching the lowers.
• Angulation of puppies' leg joints, their body length, feet and hock positioning, and pastern strength are quickly recognized by experienced breeders.

Those important points are easily overlooked by the average, novice puppy shopper, hence the importance of seeing the parents and adult offspring of the animals you are considering.

Choose your Akita carefully.

Quality

For the purposes of this discussion, the *quality* of a particular dog doesn't refer to its health or its merit as a pet. Rather, we're speaking of its probable dollar market value, and its showing and breeding potential. The quality designations used here are: show dogs, breeding stock, and pets.

Show Dogs

Show-quality animals are those that meet the breed standard in nearly all categories; they are the Akitas that bring home the ribbons and trophies from dog shows. In every breed, there are few show-quality puppies found in any given litter, even when both parents are winners. An experienced breeder might choose one or two pups from a litter to reserve for potential showing. Choosing show-quality pups is an inexact science, and requires expertise that breeders develop only after extensive experience and practice. Some breeders can pick the show-quality pup out of a litter at eight

weeks, but this talent is not easily obtained and comes only after raising dozens of litters.

The reservoir of show-quality pups is quite small in any breed, since no one is able to produce a perfect dog. Often, those puppies that seem to approach the breed standard are sold when they are older. They obviously command higher prices than pet-quality puppies, due to their rarity. Ethical breeders will usually be reticent about designating a weanling Akita as show quality. Only after a certain amount of growth and development is there any degree of certainty that the pup is outstanding, nearing perfection, and likely to be a winner. Even then, breeders and buyers alike are occasionally fooled.

Hereditary faults: Some undesirable characteristics develop later in life in any breed, and those faults can't always be foreseen at weaning age. Canine hip dysplasia (CHD), for instance, is a serious developmental, incapacitating deformity (see discussion of CHD, page 87). Over the years, dog breeders and veterinarians have tried to establish puppy examination procedures to diagnose the condition before the pups are sold. Unfortunately, the only reliable diagnostic techniques use radiographic (X-rays) examination of adults' hips.

How, then are breeders able to designate show-quality puppies, relative to hereditary, developmental faults? There are several certifying agencies that will qualify or classify X-rays of adult dogs' hips and report their findings in writing. When adults with certified-normal hips are used exclusively in breeding programs, the odds of producing puppies with normal hips are increased. Various parental certifications become important in a pup's quality designation, and it is your responsibility to ask to see those certificates. By asking to see OFA (Orthopedic Foundation for Animals) certification you can increase your odds of obtaining a totally sound dog, since over 10 percent of all Akitas have CHD.

Akitas are known to harbor a genetic possibility of ocular problems such as entropion (inward-turning eyelids), glaucoma (increased pressure within the eye), progressive retinal atrophy (wasting away of the retina), and microphthalmia (congenital small eyes).

Various autoimmune diseases such as hypothyroidism (reduced thyroid function), phemphigus foliaceus (skin disease), hemolytic anemia (loss of hemoglobin from the red blood cells), VKH (skin and eye disease), and thrombocytopenia (blood-clotting failure), are also known to exist in this breed. Epilepsy and chondrodysplasia (dwarfism) are seen in Akitas in increasing numbers.

Linebreeding: How can you be sure your Akita isn't going to develop one or more of these conditions? The best that ethical breeders can do is to have their brood stock examined and certified free of the conditions, when possible, and take extra caution when linebreeding related animals. Linebreeding refers to the breeding of distantly related individuals, and is it an accepted technique in the hands of an experienced dog breeder. It becomes dangerous only when done without serious consideration of all weaknesses of the individuals being bred, and a complete study of the pedigree of the line.

Show dogs, then, might be considered to be the cream of the Akita crop. For a potential buyer, a member of this exclusive group constitutes a considerable investment, one that is justified only if you intend to exhibit your Akita. According to the breeders contacted, if a litter has an AKC champion dam and sire, and their sires and dams are of equal quality, probably no more than one or two pups from each

Proper method of carrying an Akita.

litter is destined to be a show dog of merit. However, if dog shows aren't your cup of tea, you can get a wonderful Akita pet that won't stretch your budget quite as far.

Breeding Quality

If you have the slightest thought about breeding your Akita at some time in the future, you should undoubtedly shop for the best show-quality female available, and be prepared to devote some time and expense to showing her or hiring a professional handler to act in your behalf.

If show dogs are the cream of the Akitas, breeding animals are the cream of the show dogs. There are extremely few females that truly possess the perfection to be designated as brood bitches, and even fewer males that should be used as studs.

A well-managed bitch might hypothetically produce a litter each year for

This Akita puppy's ears aren't standing yet, and its nose-pad color is still filling in.

dog doesn't deserve the *stud dog* title.

Breeding-quality designations can't be made until the animals, male or female, are at least two years old. Until that age they haven't proven their conformation superiority by comparison with others of their sex, they can't be certified free from hereditary faults or defects, and their personalities aren't fully developed and demonstrated. When you purchase a puppy that is purported to be of show-winning quality, don't expect an ironclad guarantee!

Akita breeding is a wonderful hobby, but it should be pursued only by those who are willing and able to devote considerable study, time, and money to the endeavor. For this reason, most buyers will be discouraged from looking for show and breeding quality Akitas.

Pet Quality

This is the quality category that needs most of our attention. Akita admirers are intrigued by the outward appearance of the breed. We are fascinated by their curious facial expressions, expressive tails, sturdy bodies, and flashy colors. Our infatuation is enhanced by their temperament, physical soundness, and agility because usually, we want an Akita as a friend, companion, and playmate.

We want a beautiful, admirable pet, one that is easily recognized as a purebred Akita, but dog shows and raising pups are far from our minds. Some of us may feed our egos with framed registration certificates, and may even rave to friends about the number of champions in our pet's pedigree, but few of us are interested in showing and breeding our pets. That's a healthy situation because few dogs of any breed should be shown or bred.

Pet-quality Akitas possess the same personalities, colors, coats, and general conformation as their higher priced siblings—they just don't mea-

several years. She might contribute 50 puppies to the breed's gene pool during her breeding lifetime. A stud dog, on the other hand, might be bred dozens of times a year, and his reproductive life could be much longer. His progeny could easily number 1,000 during his breeding life. That situation is magnified by the current technology that allows sperm collection and preservation for future use, perhaps long after the contributing stud dog has died.

Those numbers are extreme, and only used to make a point. It is unlikely that any female will produce 50 puppies, or that any stud will have such a dynamic effect on the gene pool of any breed. Those sobering thoughts should, however, make you realize that most males fall short of the breeding-quality designation while they are still puppies. They only reach that lofty status after they have matured and have been consistent winners on the dog show circuit. Even then, until a fine male's progeny has proven themselves in every way, the sure up to the breed standard quite so well. Pets are likely to have more minor faults that don't bode well for a winning record in the show circuit. Those conformational or appearance faults do not denigrate the value of a companion animal. Pets' personalities, strength, or trainability shouldn't differ from those Akitas of other qualities.

Hereditary faults shouldn't be associated with pets to any greater or lesser degree than with show animals. Conscientious Akita breeders don't have some females that produce pets, and others that produce show-quality puppies. A show puppy's genetic background is the same as those of the more numerous pet siblings in a litter.

Pet quality, therefore, is the general designation that holds most of our interest. There are other advantages to buying a pet Akita besides its price. Often, breeders will part with pets from a litter at an earlier age than those they expect to be show dogs. While it's not a good idea to take puppies too young, we certainly miss a lot of fun when we acquire puppies that are several months old.

Why an Akita?

Regardless of the pet, show, or breeding potential, all Akitas require exercise. Also, consider the following:
• Does your home have ample yard space to allow your Akita to run and play?
• If your family travels a lot can your Akita go with you?
• Are you willing to spend the money for regular, preventive health care that is required for all dogs?
• Are you willing to buy the best dog food available?

All of the above questions, and others, must be honestly answered in the affirmative before you ever begin shopping for your new Akita.

Use your head, not your heart, when you look for a puppy. Don't obtain a pet because it is cute as a puppy. If you don't have the space and time to devote to raising a large breed, you should buy a smaller dog. If the dominant personality of an Akita is likely to give you and your family trouble, choose another breed.

An Akita isn't the best pet for everyone. Akita ownership carries some responsibilities that aren't present with smaller, less aggressive breeds. If, however, of the hundreds of breeds you have seen and read about, you finally decide upon an Akita, you have chosen a popular dog; there were 10,661 Akitas registered with the AKC in 1995 alone. You obviously want a strong, sturdy hiking companion, or a large, faithful family pet. You have already attended a dog show or two and watched the agile Akitas parade their physical beauty. You may have fallen in love with their almost comical facial expressions, their flashy colors, or their animated carriage. The teddy bear look of Akita puppies is difficult to ignore, but don't make the mistake of buying a cuddly little pet without considering what it will be like when it grows up.

Snowball fight anyone?

The Downside of Akitas

Consider the downside of your selection. Akitas are ambitious creatures that require regular exercise. They are strong-willed dogs that need early socialization, leadership, and control, aggressive animals that aren't likely to accept the dominance of other household pets. If your personality tends to be permissive, and you often give in to the demands of others, Akitas aren't for you. They must always be considered dog- and animal-aggressive, and you must have a strong personality and physique to control them.

Use of the Akita

Having carefully considered your choice, the next stage of selection depends upon your planned use of the dog. Akitas are outdoorsy dogs. Highly ambitious, wonderfully intelligent dogs, they fit into many molds. They may be kept as companion dogs, with no other

function in life but to please their owners. It does seem a shame to relegate such a strong, working dog to the ranks of the unemployed. If your Akita is amenable to training, you can do better.

If you are considering buying an Akita to exhibit in obedience trials, think carefully about your selection. Although clever and trainable, an Akita probably isn't the best dog to train for formal obedience trials. Only a small percentage of Akitas can be trusted to perform the "long down" in a ring with other dogs, and with no human on the other end of their leash. Shop for a puppy that is from stock that has competed in obedience work. Begin teaching it manners as soon as it arrives in your home. Only if you can find an Akita with a kind and benevolent temperament, one that is not overly possessive or dominant, will you be successful. Such Akitas *do* exist, but they are few indeed.

If you are fortunate enough to find that dog, do you have time to devote to formal obedience training? The average Akita is reported to take longer than some other breeds to reach the stage where it can be entered in an obedience trial. It takes repetitive practice at home as well as regular class time. Your dog will love the attention, and you will be impressed with the Akita's intelligence and learning ability, but it takes a great deal of time and dedication to prepare for an obedience trial.

Choosing a Young Puppy

Regardless of how you intend to use your Akita as an adult, there are other things to consider immediately. Most new owners look forward to sharing the joys of puppyhood when they buy an Akita, but for the first few months, puppies require a great deal of personal attention and time commitment. At seven, eight, or nine weeks of age, they are the typical lovable little teddy

Akitas aren't the best dogs for obedience training.

bears, happy, fun-loving little rascals. They love to play, run, and romp with children or adults. They grow like weeds, changing from roly-poly balls of fur to gangly awkward teenagers within a few weeks. Watching the puppy mature, physically and mentally, is truly a wonderful experience, but your personal interaction during that period is essential. There's no doubt that puppies add something special to a family environment, but raising an Akita puppy isn't a spectator sport. The lessons learned during those few weeks will be retained for life.

Unfortunately, raising a puppy isn't all fun and games. Pups tend to chew things. They will pass right by a dog toy to pick up and chew an expensive shoe, if given the opportunity. Akitas are certainly no worse in that department than many other breeds—all puppies like to chew; it's programmed into their makeup. That shouldn't discourage you from obtaining a young pup, but it should warn you that your lifestyle will be affected by the presence of a new puppy. You should be prepared to pick up your personal belongings and stow them out of reach of the pup. Children should be trained to pick up their toys and clothes at the same time you are teaching the pup to confine its attention to its own toys.

Chewing is a habit that is usually only corrected by substitution. A stern reprimand should accompany each shoe-chewing (or other item of clothing) episode. Immediately following the verbal reprimand, offer the pup some attractive and appropriate toy, such as a rawhide bone or chew-stick. A toy that is expendable and cost-free for growing Akitas is an empty two liter plastic soda bottle. Those empty soda bottles can entertain a puppy for hours on end. But be sure to remove the lid and paper label, as they can be swallowed and cause a lot of trouble!

Teaching the Akita to heel.

Puppies piddle. Sometimes they make horrible messes. Akitas are easily housebroken, but for a few weeks, accidents occur more often than we would like. Housebreaking, the solution to puppy messes, is quite simple, and is discussed later in the book (see page 46). If you are considering the purchase of a puppy, be ready to clean up after it.

Obtaining an Older Dog

Have you considered obtaining an older dog? Nobody wants to start a canine relationship with a senile animal, but sometimes the best choice is an Akita between six months and two or three years old—if its past history is known. There are advantages and disadvantages to such a choice:
• Those dogs have passed the puppy disease stage.

- Their preventive health care programs are established and someone else has picked up the initial tab.
- The animals are, hopefully, leash-trained, housebroken, and with some semblance of good manners.
- Their dispositions are more obvious, and their general conformation to the Akita breed standards are easily seen.
- They may have already been spayed or neutered, eliminating yet another expense.

Even though young puppies bond quicker, Akitas of all ages will adapt to new families. Dogs are followers, and they need to be led. Specific rules must be established, rewards must be given, and gentle, consistent discipline afforded. Adult Akitas are slower to change and accept a new society than puppies, but once you gain the animal's confidence and trust, the bonds of friendship, respect, and love will be strong.

The downside of selecting an adult Akita may be the lack of history of its past. If the dog you are considering hasn't been around children, or if nothing is known of its past, and you have a family, don't take a chance. If it hasn't been well socialized and you aren't sure of its temperament, keep looking.

Adult Akitas are often available from professional breeders who have taken dogs back when buyers can't keep them. Other young adults are retained for six or eight months by Akita breeders to determine whether the animals have show-winning potential. If they don't quite measure up, they will be available for purchase, sometimes at reduced prices. Older adults may be retired early from showing and breeding programs and may be adopted by Akita enthusiasts.

If you have chosen an older Akita, even more patience, care, and love should be exercised when handling it. Its habits and personality can be modified, but during the training process, it shouldn't be pressed. Adult Akitas are stubborn creatures, and until you have established a mutual trust, training should be undertaken gradually.

Quality Time

The more time you can spend with any new Akita, the more quickly the pet will respond to your love and attention. Spending quality time with an adult, just putting it on a leash and walking in the woods, is important. Playing in the backyard will allow you to establish mutual trust. Leave the training until later.

At the risk of redundancy, an earlier statement is repeated here. Learn all you can about an older Akita before you decide to take it into your home. If it has had guard training, it's not the dog for you. Based on the opinions of breeders who were contacted, there are few adult Akitas that have been rescued from pounds and other similar situations, where nothing is known about their background, that can ever be trusted in a home with children. Akitas have a great memory, and past neglect and abuse is never forgotten.

Which Sex to Choose

If you are shopping for a pet that will be neutered at or before maturity, its sex is somewhat irrelevant. Females should be spayed at about five or six months of age, and males can be castrated at that age as well. Neutered males and spayed females are equally amicable pets. Males are often larger with heavier bone structure, but female Akitas are also strong, sturdy animals.

The cost of surgically spaying a female is usually slightly higher than the castration fee, but the difference is not significant. Contrary to some opinions, castrated males and spayed females do *not* get fat because they have been neutered. As with other animals, dogs become obese because they consume more calories than they burn.

Most canines of either sex are what we make of them. If owners are rough with them as puppies, as adult dogs they will lose their inherent gentleness. If you are considerate, and treat them with loving-kindness, they reflect that quality in their personalities, no matter what their sex may be. If you display a short temper, they will probably do likewise. If you spend time with them, showing them what you want, they will respond in a positive manner. In pet ownership, patience and kindness aren't virtues—they are necessities.

If you are looking for a show dog, either sex might be appropriate. Both sexes are shown, but some breeders feel that it is easier to win AKC championships with fine males than with females of about equal quality. If you think you would like to raise puppies, naturally you must choose a female. If showing and raising puppies aren't your primary considerations, find the best representative of the breed that you can afford, and buy it.

If you give your dog love and respect, you will receive the same in return.

Sources

Breeders: The best sources for your new Akita are professional breeders. They can easily be located by attending a dog show in your area. Shows are advertised in a local newspaper, or *Akita World* magazine. All-breed shows are advertised in the *AKC Gazette* or *Dog World*. Contact a nearby Akita club for more specific information about upcoming shows and puppy matches. Lists of kennels offering puppies and adults are published in each issue of *Akita World* (see page 94 for addresses).

Another source for a pet Akita might be newspaper advertisements, but be careful! Charlatans, as well as ethical breeders often run newspaper ads, and you should be cautious when you answer them. Backyard breeders with absolutely no knowledge of the breed standards also use newspaper ads to peddle their Akitas.

Puppy mills: Puppy factories use newspaper ads to promote their puppies. Of all the mistakes you might make in your Akita selection process, the most regrettable error you could commit would be to buy from a puppy mill.

Puppies that are produced in mills may be eligible for registration, and are sold to unsuspecting buyers as fine representatives of the breed, but be aware that the mill replenishes its breeding stock from its own production, further diminishing the quality of the bloodlines.

Usually, a good look at a mill's facilities and its breeding stock will discourage you from starting your Akita experience with a pup from such a production plant. Because of the

Akitas near weaning age at play.

expense involved, preventive health measures are foregone in favor of economical mass production. Sanitation is often poor, puppies are thin and weak, breeding animals are overworked and under exercised, and the chances of attaining a good Akita are somewhere between poor and nonexistent.

Here is an example: An Akita buyer spent $900 for a six-week-old puppy mill pup. He received a ten-day money-back guarantee. The puppy's ears never stood, its testicles remained undescended, and as an adult it was crippled from hip dysplasia. Its temperament was less than desirable, and after biting several people it had to be destroyed. The hapless owner had no recourse.

If you aren't sure whether or not a newspaper ad originated from a puppy factory, or a professional, ethical breeder, make a personal visit and ask lots of questions. If the facility produces several breeds of dogs, has no evidence of dog show activity, and

offers puppies at low prices without return privileges, it's probably a mill. If the proprietors are reluctant to have you tour the facility, refuse to let you see the pups with their dam, and are vague about the quality of the puppies, run, don't walk, to the nearest exit.

Pet shops: If you find that the best or only source of an Akita puppy is the neighborhood pet shop, be sure the proprietors provide you with the same information that would be obtained from the breeder. The vaccination and health records, pedigree, and registration are important, but nothing is more vital than knowing the kind of home and environment the Akita puppy previously enjoyed. It must be well socialized, and should have spent the first seven weeks of its life with its mother and siblings.

Personality

Although difficult to evaluate in young puppies, temperaments are hereditary to a great degree. Behavior can be modified, but there seems to be a personality link from one generation to the next within a bloodline.

When choosing a companion, pay special attention to its disposition or temperament. Personalities aren't cast in stone at the time of birth, but certain traits can be found early in life. If you are shopping for a newly weaned Akita, try to select a pup that is somewhat independent, curious, and playful. If all the puppies in the litter are still sleeping in a heap beside their mother, and upon waking, they tend to seek the warmth and security of their dam, they are too young to take from her. If they tug at toys, romp about, and show more interest than apprehension when you approach, they are probably about ready for new homes. Don't choose an Akita pup because of its color or markings if it displays aggression or a timid, reclusive personality. If a pup hides from you and shies from your hand, it is either too young to separate from its siblings, or it is slow to socialize. Wait a couple of weeks and visit again.

As a final test for your Akita puppy, cradle it upside down in your arms for a few minutes. If it is content to lie there, while you reassure it, it is probably going to socialize well, and should make a good pet. If it struggles and continually tries to escape, better try another puppy, or delay your selection a week or two.

Meet the Parents

Before choosing a puppy, gain an introduction to its parents and spend some time with them. If any other close relatives are available, handle them as well. If a parent displays timidity, fear, or overt aggressiveness, you should be looking elsewhere for your new companion. If, after being around an adult Akita for an hour, you are not comfortable with it, you probably won't be comfortable with one of its offspring.

Be aware that the dam will be protective of her puppies toward strangers. Once she is called from her brood, and introduced formally to the visitors, she should calm down and proudly show her family. The dam will look her worst. She will have lost her luxurious coat, she will be thinner than usual, and will look somewhat saggy and baggy. Don't let that frighten you. It is normal for a milk-producing dam to lose condition at weaning time.

Health Status

Conformation perfection is rarely attainable in any dog, regardless of age. It's likely that some minor fault in its physical makeup, markings, or carriage will be found. Likewise, personalities often need some minor adjustments to attune them to their new owners. Those imperfections can be accepted and corrected, but health is not a negotiable commodity.

Socialization and trust make for a good pet.

Signs of Health Problems

When you visit a breeder to look at puppies, pay particular attention to the overall, general appearance of the animals you see. If any are coughing or sneezing, beware. If there is evidence of diarrhea or vomiting in the kennel area, good health is suspect.

Stages of visible illness in a puppy.

31

A happy Akita, ready for a walk.

A happy litter of Akita puppies at play.

If one or more puppies in a litter have ocular or nasal discharges, they may be in trouble. If puppies are inactive, lethargic, or appear drowsy, illnesses may be present.

When puppies are weaned and ready for new homes, they are usually examined by the breeder's veterinarian. Ask to see the health charts for the litter. Ask questions if any symptoms of illnesses are noted on the health records. Ask for vaccination records and scrutinize them closely. If the breeder has personally administered vaccinations, ask to see the manufacturer's labels for the products used. Never agree to take a puppy home that "isn't feeling well" with the breeder's promise that if it isn't better tomorrow, you can return it.

Finally, if you are suspicious about the health of your prospective Akita, wait a week and look at it again. Once you accept responsibility for the life and care of a companion, you must do whatever is necessary to maintain good health for the rest of the animal's life, but in the beginning, you are entitled to a pup in perfect health.

Signs of Good Health

Signs of a healthy puppy include curiosity, active playing with siblings, and a hearty appetite. A robust Akita has bright eyes with no cloudiness or discharge, a moist, dark nose pad, and bright pink oral mucous membranes. It should have a shiny, clean coat with no evidence of feces on the tail or the hair around the anus. Handle the puppy. It should have a supple skin texture that snaps back in place when it is gently pinched up in a fold over the withers. If the fold of skin remains pinched up after it has been released, that is evidence of dehydration and is a sign of health or nutritional problems. Its coat should be soft with no evidence of hairless areas. An Akita puppy's head and tail should be elevated, not droopy. An energetic tongue on one end, and an equally animated tail on the other, are signs of good health.

The nutritional status of a puppy is usually quite evident, even to novices. Try to visit the litter at feeding time. If the puppies attack their food with enthusiasm, that is another sign of physical and mental maturity and normal health. Be sure to ask the breeder for the feeding schedule for your new dog. Both the exact name and amount of food used, and the times the dogs are being fed are essential.

Veterinarians

Prior to purchasing any pet, choose a veterinarian. Ask questions about the veterinary hospital, staff, and facilities. Arrange to take a tour, and establish a professional relationship with your Akita's doctor. Akitas normally experience few health problems, but there will be times when you need professional assistance and advice. It is far easier to seek answers or recommendations from a clinician with whom you have established a comfortable relationship. When you find a veterinarian who seems to know your breed, ask him or her about their experience with OFA X-rays, knowledge of eye certification, and other problems you might run into.

Anticipate expenses for vaccinations, examinations, worm diagnosis and therapy, an occasional bout of diarrhea, heartworm preventive programs, flea and tick programs, and elective surgery such as spaying and neutering.

Either immediately before you purchase an Akita, or at the time it is taken to your home, it should be examined by a veterinarian. If no exam has been done at the time the pup is available, strike an agreement with the breeder. Meet the breeder and puppy at your veterinarian's office, and, after the puppy has been examined in your presence and pro-

Regular veterinary checkups are vital.

nounced healthy and free of discernible congenital defects, finalize the sale. If a breeder refuses to cooperate with that plan, there is probably a reason, and you should consider looking elsewhere for your Akita. The cost of the examination is usually borne by the buyer if it is done at your request, but an examination fee is a modest investment when considering

"I'm Akita Banana and I've come to say..."

the lifetime relationship that depends on beginning with a healthy pet!

When a new dog of any age is examined, the veterinarian should be furnished with a complete history of the animal's diet, vaccinations, worm tests, and all treatments that have been rendered for illnesses. The parents' eye certification, and hip certification should be examined by the veterinarian, and those documents should be explained to you. With that information and the results of the professional examination, your veterinarian will make specific recommendations for future preventive health care.

Breeder's Guarantees

Sometimes, foolish guarantees are requested by buyers. For instance, there is no way that a breeder can guarantee that your new puppy will win in puppy matches and shows, or that it will breeze its way to AKC championship.

A puppy can't be guaranteed to be free of all parasites, since some remain dormant for extended periods of time. Guarantees of good health are only effective as long as the breeder has control of the puppy's nutrition and environment. Once your Akita arrives in your home, its nutrition and health are your responsibility. If you make rapid dramatic changes in its diet, digestive problems are likely to occur.

A breeder *can* guarantee that a pup has been given its first vaccination of the series, but a single vaccination doesn't provide immunity to communicable diseases unless the necessary booster vaccinations are given at the appropriate times.

Valuable guarantees are offered by some professional breeders. They may guarantee to take the dog back if it doesn't work out in your home. They may refund your purchase price or some portion of it, and there may

be time limitations on that guarantee. *Any guarantee offered must be in writing.*

The Take-Back Guarantee

Many ethical Akita breeders offer lifetime return privileges to buyers of their purebred dogs. Those breeders will either keep the returned pet or they will try to place it in a suitable home.

Circumstances change: A home is sold or traded for an apartment, finances change, illness, a death in the family, a divorce, or remarriage may change your lifestyle. New, real-life situations may suddenly preclude the ownership of a large, dominant, outdoor dog.

Sometimes people buy an Akita on impulse. They are unaware of the temperament or size of the breed. When the rotund, furry little teddy bear grows up, the owners aren't ready for the 100 pounds (45 kg) of aggression they now possess. Or, they haven't devoted enough time to the care and education of a large dog.

The Akita that becomes an unwanted pet should not end up in an animal shelter or pound. If you are unable to keep your Akita, your first call should be to the breeder from whom you purchased your pet. If you bought it from a pet store, the puppy may have been acquired from a responsible breeder who will help.

If the source of your Akita isn't responsive to your problem, the next call should be to a nearby Akita breeder. Their names and phone numbers are listed, arranged by state, in the back of each *Akita World* newsletter, which is published every other month, and is available by subscription, or at dog shows (see address on page 94).

Professional Akita breeders can put you in contact with breed clubs that sponsor rescue groups whose mission if is to find homes for unwanted

Akitas. The name and addresses of Akita breed clubs may also be obtained from the AKC.

It's no sin to find yourself in a situation in which you can't keep your pet, but it is unconscionable to deny your stewardship responsibility and dump the Akita at the nearest animal shelter. All dogs deserve better treatment than that, but especially an Akita.

Reputable breeders have been known to guarantee an animal's ability to place well in dog shows, providing it is handled by a professional. Some progressive breeders might offer you a show-dog guarantee, which might offer to replace the puppy or furnish another—with certain neutering stipulations for the first dog—if the dog is less than advertised. That type of guarantee is fine, providing you have the facilities to house both dogs. The same type of document might be written to guarantee that an eight-week-old puppy will mature without any hereditary deformities.

Registration

Every purebred dog, regardless of age or sex, can be registered if the breed is acknowledged by the registry and if both parents were registered (except where the parents have a limited AKC registration).

If a prospective seller states that an Akita is purebred but can't be registered, be suspicious. If in doubt, call the AKC. Even though an Akitas' appearance is quite distinctive, it is possible that a mixed-breed dog could resemble a purebred Akita. Backyard breeders may produce puppies from purebred, pet-quality Akitas that were purchased from breeders who withheld registration papers.

When a litter is born to AKC-registered parents, the AKC furnishes separate puppy registration papers for each puppy in the litter (see Litter Registration, page 90). That puppy registration document should accompany the puppy, providing no contrary agreements are made between buyer and seller. As mentioned above, registration documents for pet-quality pups may be held by the breeder until the buyer furnishes proof that the pup was castrated or spayed. Limited registration may be implemented, or the breeder may insist on co-ownership to control future breeding. You as buyer, should be aware that those precautions are being taken, and you should agree with them, in writing.

Bringing Your Akita Home

It is important to handle and treat your Akita puppy in the same way as you propose to handle the adult. If the adult, 100-pound (45 kg) Akita is to be kept outdoors, start the new puppy outdoors. When a puppy is raised for the first few months in the house, then confined to the yard, it will often become destructive. It may begin excessive digging, chewing trees, and generally making a nuisance of itself.

It is also of vital interest to begin its socialization with friends and neighbors as soon as possible after the puppy has had its vaccinations.

This three week old puppy may be a future champion.

A Puppy in the House

Your new Akita puppy is probably destined to be a family pet, and will spend a good deal of time inside your house. Perhaps you already have a fenced yard and expect the puppy to have the run of the yard and sleep in your home at night. Those accommodations are fine, providing you have taken a few preliminary precautions to protect both your puppy and your property.

A Puppy in the Yard

If you have a fenced yard, the puppy-proofing task is easier, but don't relax until you have once again done a hazard inventory:
• Your fence may leave something to be desired. If constructed of wood, it is chewable. If it doesn't go all the way to the ground, it may only serve to teach your pup to dig out.
• Garden hoses may be attacked and punctured if they are not hung out of reach of the venturesome little Akita.
• Gardening chemicals, including fertilizers and insecticides, present major problems to pups. They may chew on a bag, box, or sprayer hose, ingesting small amounts of toxic chemicals. All such products should be put well out of reach of your new Akita.
• Fertilizers and insecticides that have been recently applied to the lawn or garden should be watered well into the soil to prevent puppies from contaminating their feet, then licking off the toxins. And when watering after application of lawn chemicals, be sure not

to allow the puppy to drink from pools or puddles that form on sidewalks.
• Labels on the packages tell you of the danger of garden products. If your pup has chewed and possibly consumed the contents, call your veterinarian immediately. Give him or her the label ingredients and the amount consumed, if it can be ascertained. Don't attempt to treat the puppy on your own unless efforts to obtain professional help have failed. Keep in mind that the puppy is quite small and has a rapid metabolic rate, which makes the danger even greater, and the need to get immediate help more demanding.
• Antifreeze has a sweet taste that dogs usually like. It contains a kidney toxin that can kill your dog, and, unfortunately, treatment is not terribly effective, even when the poisoning is discovered early. Therefore, *keep all antifreeze out of reach of dogs*. This isn't just a puppy problem, but can affect adults as well. In case antifreeze poisoning is suspected, waste no time in obtaining professional help.
• Windshield washer fluid, and other alcohol products are equally dangerous. Virtually all automotive chemicals can be extremely hazardous to dogs' health. Don't leave oils, greases, or other products where your Akita pup can reach them.
• Paint, turpentine, paint thinner, and acetone should be stored well out of the dog's reach. Paint removers are particularly dangerous, and even a quick investigative lick can cause severe tongue burns. A clumsy puppy might tip a can over while looking for something to do, and find its feet bathed in the caustic stuff. In the event that happens, rinse the feet immediately with gallons of cool water. Then wash its feet off with soap and water and call your veterinarian.

• Swimming pools can be hazardous to the life of your new Akita. All dogs are able to swim, but some pools are constructed with escape ladders that only humans can use. If you have such a pool, provide a means of escape for your dog before it is allowed to go near the pool. Show the puppy where the steps are, and drill it several times in the use of them.

If the foregoing discussion leaves you with the impression that Akita puppies are animated, relentless, destructive forces, please understand that these are worst case scenarios. Akita puppies are no more mischievous than any other pups, and most Akita youngsters are not bent on destruction. All puppies indulge in activities that land them in trouble once in a while. By identifying hazards, you might save your puppy's life, or at least you may save yourself some money.

Puppies often learn to entertain themselves.

HOW-TO:
Puppy-Proofing Your Home

Healthy puppies are rather destructive little creatures, and Akitas are no exception. Before a puppy is left alone in your home for more than a few minutes, you should do a quick hazard inventory. Familiar objects that are safe for the family may present some degree of danger to a new puppy. Look around for some of the following household puppy hazards:

• Low hanging telephone or computer cords make wonderful tug-of-war toys for a pup, but unfortunately, the wires usually don't last long and may be difficult to replace. They are also dangerous should they be wrapped around the puppies' necks.

• Draperies and curtains that swing at the puppy's eye level are also quite challenging and may be attacked without provocation and pulled down or torn.

Plant eating may be dangerous to the puppy's health.

• Household electrical appliance cords are dangerous, and those that are accessible to the puppy should be unplugged when the pup is left unsupervised even for a few minutes.

• Cords that are unplugged to prevent electrical shock but left hanging can also be dangerous for puppies. Dangling cords attached to irons, toasters, radios, and other appliances are prime targets for puppy attacks. An electric mixer and its contents, mashed all over the kitchen floor, is a hapless reminder that all cords should be coiled and put well out of the reach of your Akita puppy.

• Household chemicals are sometimes accessible to an adventuresome pup. Items such as oven cleaner, laundry soap, bleach, dishwashing detergent, insecticides, and other items that are frequently kept beneath the kitchen sink are an ever-present danger to puppies.

• Scrubbers such as steel wool and plastic coils are, for whatever reason, attractive to puppies and can be chewed up and swallowed.

• Sponges are particularly hazardous; they are attractive to pups, and if swallowed, can require surgical removal.

In case your puppy does get into a cupboard, try to ascertain what chemicals may have been swallowed, read the labels, and watch the pup carefully for signs of illness such as lethargy, vomiting, and diarrhea. If you notice these signs, call your veterinarian. In the case of a swallowed sponge, the signs of illness will be vomiting food shortly after eating.

Trying to make a long distance call.

Houseplants and Other Dangers

Houseplants are another class of attractive targets for puppy attacks. Plant dangers are threefold:

1. Most potted plants can't defend themselves from a puppy encounter and usually lose the conflict and their lives.

2. Messy, damp potting soil, mixed with shreds of leaves, stems, and roots, spread all over the floor, may be all that remains of a once beautiful philodendron.

3. Some plants are poisonous, and can cause serious illnesses in dogs. Philodendron, poinsettia, and a variety of other common house plants are toxic to some degree.

Also watch out for the following:

• Encounters with artificial foliage, whether poisonous or nontoxic, may upset puppies' stomachs, resulting in vomiting and diarrhea. The gastric upset is usually self-limiting and easily treated, but the cleanup chore is not a pleasant one.

• Lower bookshelves might attract the puppy as a potpourri of leather and paper toys. Books are expensive chew toys for pups, and should be protected.

• Wastebaskets are fair game for an ambitious puppy, and the wads of paper and tissues found in them make wonderful toys.

• Because children's rooms usually contain an abundance of balls, plastic toys, seashells, dolls, and other gimcracks and gewgaws, it's a good idea to keep the doors to those rooms closed against puppy invasion. A small jacks ball may look harmless enough, but an Akita puppy is big enough to swallow the little sponge rubber ball. It won't go through the pyloric opening of the stomach into the small intestine, and unless it is retrieved quickly, it will require surgical removal.

• Tablecloths, doilies, and coffee table scarves that hang over the tables' edges may be tug-of-war targets for your new Akita pup.

• Throw rugs and throw pillows, especially those with tassels, also provide great fun and entertainment for your Akita pup.

Dangerous chemicals are a hazard to puppies.

A puppy's attraction to an item seems to be directly proportional to its replacement cost. For some unknown reason, old, worn-out shoes aren't as likely to be chewed as brand new ones. Also, the children's favorite toys or your most expensive gloves are always the ones that suffer the most abuse.

Solutions

If the pup is to spend much time in the house, it makes good sense to put up a couple of infant gates on doorways to limit your Akita's roaming to one or two rooms.

A portable dog pen will serve the same purpose, and can be moved from room to room. Such pens are available from any pet supply store and are much less expensive than the valuable items they protect.

Crating the pup is another way to protect and control it for the first few weeks in a new home.

Puppy-proofing a house isn't easy; sometimes it's impossible. Perhaps the best way to save your valuables from destruction is to confine the pup to the yard. This, of course, doesn't allow you to housebreak your Akita; that brings us back to the suggestion of a portable pen, or a crate.

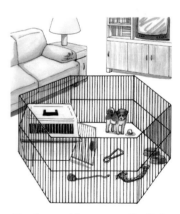

Confinement for a puppy the first few days.

It's dinner time.

Bonding with Your Akita

Human bonding and family adjustment occurs rapidly in young puppies. The period between three weeks and three months of age is the most important human bonding time for Akitas. During that brief period they form life-long relationships with their human companions. Akitas acquired before three months will accept correction quickly and easily, and the lessons offered will be promptly imprinted on the personalities of those youngsters. That is the prime time to establish your love and devotion to your new pet, and it will reciprocate.

The time spent with your Akita puppy is important, to you, and to the pet. Responding to your care and attention, it learns the rules of the household. At the same time, you learn something of its character, its likes and dislikes, and the things that satisfy it the most. You can use this knowledge later, when more specific training is initiated.

As it gradually outgrows its beaver-like need to chew, your Akita will absorb the family's routine and the restrictions placed upon it. Within a few weeks, it is anxious to please. Always playful, it begins to learn to recognize its own toys and to anticipate the Frisbee games and hide-and-seek exercises. Have patience—puppies do grow up!

After the vaccination program is finished, the socialization process must begin. The more you can get your Akita puppy in contact with other people and their pets, the better. When your Akita is about four months old, you should make a concentrated effort to take it on walks in the park, to the mall, or wherever people and dogs are easily encountered. If at that age the dog growls at humans, contact a professional trainer or the breeder who raised it for advice.

Akita puppies love to be in the yard, so make sure yours is puppy-proof.

Spending time in the yard with your Akita (or Akitas) is important.

Keeping Your Akita Healthy

If you weren't present at your puppy's examination, call the veterinarian and talk with him or her. Or better yet, take your new Akita to your veterinarian for another evaluation. Ask questions about the dog's future vaccination requirements, and be sure to jot down the recommendations offered. Obtain advice about parasite control, including both internal, external, and circulatory parasites. Ask about Lyme disease, valley fever, or other exotic diseases that may be endemic in your area.

This early appointment with your veterinarian is an excellent time to discuss spaying or castration of pets. Also, if you anticipate boarding your Akita at any time, ask for kennel referrals. If you aren't sure you can clip your pet's nails, ask the professional to teach you. Inquire about the availability of emergency treatment for your pet. If the veterinarian doesn't take emergency calls, obtain the name of the nearest and best emergency clinic. The relationship you establish with your veterinarian at this time should endure for years. It is to your advantage to begin the communication by asking questions and following advice. A sound and open relationship with your veterinarian is the best insurance policy you can get for your Akita.

Feeding Your Akita

The records you received with your Akita should contain dietary information, listing the name of the food being fed, the frequency of meals, and the quantity fed at each meal. Supplements are rarely necessary, but if they have been used, their brand names should also be given.

When you take the puppy home, minimize the stress of environmental change by following the previously established feeding program. Even if you wish to change the diet to a better quality food, that change should not

The Akita is truly a dog for all seasons.

be made immediately. After a week or two in your home, you can begin dietary changes if desired, but make those changes slowly by mixing the new product with the previous food in gradually increasing amounts. A total diet change should take at least one week, perhaps longer.

An elevated temperature is the sign of illness.

An accident about to happen.

Providing a Kennel and Run

If your situation is one that invites the construction of an Akita kennel, choose an area that slopes gently downward from front to back. A few inches or even a foot of slope makes for good drainage away from the front of the run, where the dog spends most of its time. That is particularly important if your home has a rainy environment. A 6 foot (2 m) chain-link fence will serve your needs well. Make the run as large as the space and your pocketbook will allow, and if you have a choice, make it longer rather than wider to allow for a maximum of exercise.

Most kennel runs are not adequate to provide ample exercise space for an athletic Akita, and should be used only as a place to safely house your pet when you are away. The run should be large enough to allow the dog to move about freely, and it should be located where shade from the sun is always available.

An elevated wooden platform should be built, large enough to allow your adult Akita to stretch out in a dry area. The platform should be high enough to keep the dog out of the mud. If you live in an area where snow or rain prevails, it's best to put some type of cover over the platform to help keep it dry. If you live in hot, dry country, a sun screen is essential.

The Doghouse

Koby will also need a doghouse. Commercial, molded, fiberglass doghouses are available in sizes to fit an Akita. They are expensive, but should be a one-time investment. When shopping for a doghouse for a small puppy, it's sometimes difficult to remember that puppies grow up. Don't make the mistake of buying or building a house that is going to be too small for a 100-pound (45 kg) adult Akita. The dome-shaped, igloo types and more conventional rectangular fiberglass houses both have removable bottoms to facilitate cleaning.

Note: There is one fact you must keep in mind: While yards or kennels provide the opportunity for exercise, they don't provide the initiative. They give your pet freedom, but it's your responsibility to see that Koby gets the exercise he needs.

A kennel provides security for your Akita.

Fences

Naturally, if your Akita sleeps in your home, elaborate outdoor housing is unnecessary; however, a word of caution: If your yard fence is only 3 feet (91.4 cm) tall, it's probably not high enough to contain an energetic and adventuresome Akita. Such a yard is great when the family is with the dog, but if left alone behind a short fence, boredom or curiosity may stimulate your dog to jump, and such a fence would be no challenge for a strong, athletic Akita adult. The same applies to wooden fences that are easily dug under, or destroyed by gnawing teeth.

Traveling by Car with Your Akita

Hopefully, your Akita's only relationship with cars will be as a backseat passenger. Far too many dogs are injured when following their owners' automobiles, chasing cars, or running into street traffic. Few domestic canines have any great fear of riding in cars. If your pet is frightened by the engine noise or the vehicle's motion, patience and short trips will gradually condition it to the engine noise and car movement.

It is important to make your Akita behave while riding in a car, whether or not any fear is involved. You decide where you want Koby to ride, and insist that he stay in the designated area. Dog safety harnesses are available in pet supply stores. They fasten into the automobile's seat belt system and hold the pet in a fairly confined area of the car. If space allows, a crate should be used for all traveling with your Akita. It is a safer and more positive means of confinement. *Don't put your Akita in a crate in the car's trunk!*

Motion sickness is always a messy business. Salivating vomiting, and signs of abdominal discomfort all accompany car sickness. If your pet suffers from this malady, your veterinarian or the drugstore can furnish some Dramamine, Bonamine, or other motion sickness tablets. The dosage varies according to the size and age of the dog and, although most are relatively safe, you should check the product dosage with your veterinarian. In time, the puppy may outgrow the problem, but until then, give a dose of the drug about an hour before your car trip. It beats cleaning up the mess afterward.

Anyone who drives a pickup truck is bound to consider allowing the Akita to ride in the back. Fight the urge! If you insist, cross-tie the dog so it is impossible for it to leave the moving vehicle. Then periodically consult a veterinarian about your dog's eyes, as they are bound to be abused by the dust and debris flying about.

A spacious, secure yard is the best place for your Akita to play.

If your Akita spends time in the woods consider asking your veterinarian about flea and tick control programs.

Even a junkyard dog should be properly housebroken.

If you live in a city, it is important to find a park or other open area where you can exercise your Akita.

Training Your Akita

Now comes the fun part of Akita owning. If approached gently and positively, and in short sessions, training is a rewarding experience. In the beginning, all of the training attempts will seem like wasted time. The puppy will become obstinate, sit down, drag its feet, and refuse to listen or cooperate. Have patience. Take your time. What isn't learned today will be picked up tomorrow. Others have done this; certainly you can do it too.

The Importance of Obedience Training

All companion dogs will benefit from obedience training, but it is even more important in dominant breeds such as Akitas—you owe it to yourself and your neighbors to train your Akita! Apply common sense to your training; don't train the dog in a haphazard, off-again, on-again manner. Have a plan in mind, and stick to it. If you attend classes with a qualified instructor, you can train Koby yourself. Sending him off to a professional trainer is often a mistake; Koby will perform beautifully for the trainer, but won't do anything for you. You live with the dog—to get the desired response, you should train him yourself.

If other members of the family want him to be obedient to them, they should be involved with his education. Akitas are wonderfully loyal family dogs, and if the adult family members are all involved with training the dog, they will appreciate his knowledge and ability. They will learn what to expect from him.

Do dogs want to be trained? Probably not. The trick to training your Akita is to make the endeavor enjoyable. They delight in regular social interaction with humans. If a behavior is pleasant for the Koby while he is involved with it, he will repeat it in the future. Give the dog time to learn; don't press him. Watch him carefully and see what exercises are most agreeable to him, and repeat them more frequently. Akitas have long memories, but puppies' attention spans are quite short. Perhaps your companion will never volunteer for training, but if it's enjoyable, the dog won't fight it.

Ready to learn.

Crate Training

Many people cringe at the thought of crating their Akita; they can't imagine a big, athletic dog being confined to a crate. If used properly, the crate is an excellent and harmless way to manage your puppy and can be used in certain cases when it becomes an adult. Of course, you should never keep your Akita in a crate for hours on end, but only when necessary.

• Obtain a large size fiberglass crate, with adequate ventilation. As in choosing doghouses, don't make the mistake of buying a crate to fit a puppy, as one day soon, your Akita will be quite a large dog and the crate should accommodate it as a grown-up.

• Keep some article of your clothing, or the puppy's favorite toy in the crate together with a blanket or rug.

• Confine the pup to the crate for short periods of time in the beginning, but always leave the door open when not being used.

• Don't tease the dog. When you crate it, walk away and pay no attention. If the dog barks, respond with a sharp "*No*," and continue with your work.

• Be sure to take the puppy out of the crate frequently for eliminations.

Regular sessions of crating the puppy will result in acceptance of the crate as the puppy's own den, and it will soon return there for naps or when the activity of the household becomes irritating. It will become a favorite place, one that is quiet and secluded.

When housebreaking your Akita, a crate can be used instead of a wire pen to confine the pup. It is also a great help when traveling, and is preferable to a seat belt to confine your pet in your car. It can be used to house the dog when neighbor children are visiting, until they can be properly introduced to the dog and the dog becomes used to them. A crate is also a sure way to prevent confrontations in the case of visiting dogs.

Never use the crate as a negative reinforcement in training—it should not be a means of punishment for doing something wrong. It is a good idea to give the dog some special treat when it enters the crate, and another when it is taken out. If you make crating a positive experience, your Akita will not resent it.

Housebreaking

Akitas are fastidious, almost catlike in their excretions. Most will housebreak themselves if given the opportunity. They are extremely clean and don't want to soil their living space. Nevertheless, housebreaking is a subject that must be discussed, even if your dog is destined to live outside most of the time.

Puppies use little discretion, and when they feel the urge to urinate or defecate, they hardly hesitate in their play. It's done and over with before you notice it; then it's too late to correct. A professional dog trainer has estimated that your response to an "accident" must be within five seconds from the time it happens, or the puppy will not connect your corrective action with its mistake.

Rules to Follow

The first rule is to always take the pup to the same area of the yard for its eliminations. Once the odors of previous eliminations are established in the toilet area, the pup will seek out that spot when necessary. Take it to the designated toilet area immediately after each meal, when it wakes in the morning, after naps, and before bedtime at night. If you are able to train yourself to that task, the pup will be housebroken before you know it.

For the first week or so, don't let the pup out of your sight when indoors. Each time it squats to urinate or defecate, say "*No*," pick it up and carry it to the toilet area. Even if it has started to urinate or defecate, it should be carried outside to finish. You can't allow it to finish on the floor, then carry it outside. To do so will only train the pup to take a trip to the outdoors after each elimination. After it has emptied its bladder or bowel, praise the pup and allow it back inside.

Negative Approaches

Don't use a negative approach to housebreaking. A pup has no way of knowing our customs, and to punish, scold, or reprimand a puppy for messing on the floor is a mistake. To the Akita pup, its eliminations are perfectly natural, and the particular placement of those eliminations is irrelevant. If you swat the pup when it is performing a natural act, you will only confuse it. Rubbing its nose in the eliminations is equally confusing. Once the urination or defecation is completed, it's gone from the animal's mind within seconds. Remember the five-second rule: Respond to an accident within five seconds.

The Best Tools

Prevention, substitution, and positive reinforcement are the best tools to use in housebreaking. If you never let you pup out of your sight, you can prevent it from messing on the floor. When it shows signs of turning in circles, in preparation for moving its bowels, pick it up quickly and substitute the toilet area of the yard for your carpet. When you first see it squat to urinate, quickly pick it up and carry it outside. When it follows directions and eliminates in the appropriate place, praise and reward the pup. Patience is required, but persistence will pay off in the long haul.

Introducing the Collar and the Leash

As with housebreaking, leash training is a part of good manners that all dogs should learn. The leash is an excellent way to assume the alpha leader role in the pack. It should be started as early as possible, and pursued with diligence throughout the dog's life.

Although there are as many methods of leash training as there are dog trainers, one fact is fundamental: A positive approach should be taken. An Akita puppy is an easy subject; Koby wants to follow you anyway, and adding a collar and leash doesn't add much stress to his little body and mind.

The Collar

A buckle collar, made of leather or nylon web, is available in the correct size at the pet supply store. It should be snug, but not tight. If you are investing in a collar for a young pup, buy one large enough to allow growth.

Your new pup should be introduced to its collar as soon as possible, but for the first two or three days, the collar shouldn't be left on Koby when he is alone for long periods of time. After a few days of wearing the collar, he will tire of trying to scratch it off, and will ignore it. At that point, it is usually safe to leave the collar on full time.

Correct choke collar placement.

47

To compete in novice obedience, an Akita must learn to stand for examination by the judge.

Now you can exercise Koby out of the yard, and the new experiences, smells, and sights are reward enough for the restriction of the collar and leash. Don't begin serious obedience training at first; just enjoy your pet's companionship.

From that easy beginning you can gradually progress to teaching the pup to walk on your left side, in preparation for more advanced training (see Heel, page 51).

Tags

As Koby grows, the buckle collar should be replaced with a larger size. It should be left on him all the time, with tags attached for identification. Tags are available through any pet supply shop. Order one with your name, address, and telephone number, and attach it securely to your Akita's collar. The best type of identification tag is one that rivets flatly to the collar on both ends. They come complete with rivets and no special application equipment is needed. That type can't be easily lost and isn't apt to catch on things when the pup is playing.

Leash Training

Hopefully, Koby has adapted to his leash, and now accepts it gracefully. It is time to remove the web or leather collar and put a chain collar in its place. Snap on a sturdy nylon web leash, and begin the first exercise.

Always use a chain collar for training. This collar is often called a "choke" collar, a misnomer if the collar is used correctly. *The chain collar should be removed when the dog is not on leash.* The chain collar is formed from a chain with a ring attached to each end, and in order to work properly, it should fit the dog. But remember, one size doesn't work for your Akita from puppyhood to adulthood. It should measure approximately 2 inches (5.1 cm) greater than the diameter of the dog's neck. To form

Chain collars should always be used for training, but for early leash work, in young puppies, the web collar is fine.

When to Begin Leash Training

It's never too early to begin leash training. As soon as the collar has ceased to annoy the pup, snap a short leash on and let Koby drag it while you add encouragement by offering a tidbit now and then. Pick up the leash and take a short walk around the yard. In the beginning, it's best to take only a few steps at a time, coaxing Koby to follow by offering tidbits from your fingers. Your companion will soon connect the tidbit rewards with the collar and leash, and will welcome the appearance of the leash each day. Even though it is important to let the puppy know who has control of the leash, it should be done in a positive way, *never* as punishment or correction.

48

the collar, drop the chain through one of the rings. Then attach the lead snap to the free ring. Place the collar on the dog so that the end that is attached to the leash comes up the left side of the dog and across the top of its neck. The dog is kept on your left side, and when it is necessary to correct the dog's action, the collar is given a quick tug, then released. If a chain collar is placed wrong, it will not release quickly, and may injure the dog. A chain collar that is too long will not close quickly enough to be effective. Keep in mind that the foregoing discussion assumes that the dog will be walking on your *left* side.

Training collars are available that are made of a dozen or so hinged wire prongs. The dull prongs turn against the dog's neck when the leash is tightened, and they may be an effective way of training an obstreperous adult Akita. There are other, better ways of getting a dog's attention in most cases but they should be used only by professional trainers when necessary, and when they are used, must never be abused. If you need a pronged collar to control your Akita all the time, there is probably something wrong with your training technique. Prong collars are banned from the premises of AKC shows.

Command Clarity

Separate every command into five parts, and make each part distinct and clear. Remember, your Akita has better hearing than you do, so shouting isn't going to help. Neither should the command be repeated time and again for a single function.
1. Say the dog's *name* clearly. This is difficult when the name is complex or lengthy, so if necessary, shorten the name and make it simple. When you say his name, you get Koby's attention; it lets him know that you will soon give a command that you expect to be followed.

This young Akita's attention is focused on its owner's face and hands.

2. After a brief interlude of a second or two, give the *command*.
3. After another few seconds, *enforce* the action, gently and firmly.
4. and **5.** After the action has been successfully performed, *release* him from the command and offer a *reward* with your praise.

Basic Commands

Come

Akitas must obey this command without hesitation. It is perhaps the easiest to teach your puppy and can be used in many situations and games. You will probably teach your pup to come at feeding time, without even trying. This is one exercise that can be learned by a young pup, and the sooner it is mastered, the better. It should be practiced until the pup's response is automatic.

Fasten a long lightweight nylon line to Koby's collar. Allow him to wander away from you for some distance. Then, with enthusiasm, and open arms, drop to one knee and give the command, "*Koby*, (hesitation) *come*." If Koby doesn't respond with the same enthusiasm you showed, give a tug or two on the line, repeating the command. When Koby arrives on your lap, lavish praise on him and give him a tidbit. Then release him from the exercise with an "*OK*," and continue to praise him.

Repeat this exercise frequently at odd times to catch your dog off guard. When its response to the command comes quickly, try it off leash, in the fenced yard. Repeat the command several times daily for grooming, feeding, and especially, for petting.

Never call your dog to you to scold or discipline it; that will defeat your purpose. Instead, each time it comes on command, praise and pet the dog, regardless of what mischief you have called it away from.

Sit

With your puppy at your left side, in a calm, normal voice, say "*Koby*." Wait a second before you say "*Sit*," and when that has been absorbed, push down on the pup's rump. It's important to allow a few seconds after the command is given, before the action is taken, to let the dog understand exactly what you desire. Koby must connect the command with the desired action. After you push his bottom to the ground, offer a tidbit to the dog at eye level, immediately in front of his face. This will help him to sit, and will encourage him to stay in that position. After a few seconds of sitting, release him by saying "*OK*," then praise him.

The tidbit reward is only the beginning. Praise and petting is the real reward, for both of you. Praise must be given in abundance after each suc-cessful exercise. When the pup doesn't quite get the exercise right, use the word "*Wrong*," in a conversational tone, before you make the correction. Reserve the word "*No*," in a gruff voice, for times when Koby is in trouble and you want him to refrain altogether from whatever mischief he is involved in.

Practice this exercise several times, but don't expect miracles. If you are lucky, the dog will catch on the first day, but don't count on it. Don't add to the confusion with more training at this time.

Next time, practice the *sit* command several times, and if met with success, progress to another command. If it takes several sessions to learn the *sit* command, so be it—you are in no hurry, and some dogs take longer than others to catch on to the first exercise. Usually, puppies take longer to master simple exercises than older dogs, and their attention span is always shorter.

Stay

When Koby is sitting, looking for another tidbit, tell him to *stay*, while you remain standing at his right side. If he tries to lie down or stand up, say "*Wrong*," repeat the command "*Stay*," and put him back into a sitting position. After a few seconds, tell him "*OK*," and give him a reward. Again, the command is broken into several parts: first, the dog's name, then the command, then the action, the release, and finally, the reward and praise.

When the dog has conquered the *stay* command on most occasions, try to move away from your position. When you put the leash on the ground and start to walk away, the faithful pup will try to follow. Say "*Wrong*," repeat the *stay* command, place Koby in the sitting position, and back away again. With a few tries, the pup will get the idea and stay put while you take several steps away from him, then return to finish the exercise. Don't ever forget to release him from the stay, and never finish the exercise without praise and a reward.

Some words of advice: Don't expect too much of a puppy. Take only a few steps away in the beginning. Don't push the pup to the limit and expect him to stay interminably like the dogs in an obedience trial will do. Return quickly to the pup's side, take your position with the dog on your left, pick up the leash, and release him from the stay command. Most pups are doing well if they stay for 20 seconds without fidgeting.

Down

This command is used in novice obedience trials, and is also a convenient way to let the pup relax while you talk to neighbors on your daily walks. It should be given in the same way that the *sit* command is used. Begin the exercise with the dog in the sitting or standing position. Be sure to hesitate between the dog's name and the command. "*Koby*, (hesitation) *down*," is the command. Don't muddy the issue with excess words. Never use "*Lie down*" or confuse the pup with "*Koby, sit down.*"

After you have given the *down* command, push his body to the ground, slowly and gently. Don't fight him. If necessary, hold a tidbit so low that he can't reach it without lying down. Or, if he doesn't cooperate, push him to the sitting position, and fold his elbows, placing him on his belly.

Akitas, being dominant creatures, often dislike being forced to lie down but, if the exercise is taught when they are young, accompanied by lavish praise and appropriate tidbits, that obstacle can be overcome. Once the position is reached, heap on the praise. Petting can't be overdone.

After the *down* command, say "*Stay*," and walk away for a few steps. Finish the exercise by returning to

him, releasing him from the exercise, and lauding great praise upon him. Once the dog realizes that you aren't leaving him, and if he stays you will return with more praise and tidbits, he will soon catch on.

Heel

Your Akita is already familiar with the leash, and isn't frightened by occasional tugging. Each time you bring out the leash, the pup realizes that a walk is on the agenda and soon, new vistas are to be discovered. The battle is half over.

Heeling is another exercise that all well-behaved dogs must learn. Place Koby on your left side, running the leash through your left hand, holding it with your right. Give the dog the command, "*Koby, sit.*" Then as you step off with your left foot, give the command, "*Heel*," As you walk along, keep the dog at your side with gentle tugs on the leash. If he is accustomed to running ahead of you, the biggest problem is to keep Koby at heel, and that action can be handled easily by controlling the leash.

This is a tough exercise for an ambitious puppy to master. Koby is anxious to forge ahead and investigate something at the far end of his leash. Don't hold the leash too tightly; leave enough slack for him to move a step ahead or behind you, but don't let him to bolt ahead. After he has properly heeled for a dozen steps, stop, and push his bottom to the ground to the sitting position. Then release him with an "*OK*," reward him with a tidbit, and praise. Begin the exercise all over again.

If the pup wants to lag behind, encourage him to keep up with you by teasing him along with a tidbit. Soon your Akita will be walking by your side, taking turns and stops in its stride.

A word to the wise: Heeling is fine for dog shows, for maximum control of your dog in a crowd, and when cross-

Akita at heel in a training class.

the ears and under the chin, and a tidbit, are sure ways to begin the trust relationship. When the dog responds correctly to a command, be liberal with your praise and gentle touching. Your hands should always be used to praise your Akita, never to reprimand it. A palatable treat, given with the praise and petting, will help the trusting relationship move forward even faster.

Negative reinforcement shouldn't be used with any dog, but that is especially true for an adult Akita. If you wish to show displeasure, use a gruff tone of voice, but at the usual conversational decibel level. Yelling and waving your arms is sure to invoke a defensive reaction in a new Akita. If you frighten an adult Akita, you have lost the ability to control it, and your hand, waving and threatening, is certainly at risk of being bitten.

ing busy streets—that's where it should end. Heeling is boring for Koby, and although all dogs should learn to heel, they should be given more freedom whenever the space will allow it.

Positive Reinforcement in Training the Adult Akita

If you did not obtain your Akita as a puppy but as an adult, it is most important that you use patience, kindness, and positive reinforcement as your training tools.

Use positive reinforcement to reward each task your adult Akita performs for you. Love, petting, scratching behind

Physical Correction

Any necessary physical correction should be controlled and moderate. There is no canine error that should be corrected by striking your dog. If you find it necessary to physically discipline your adult Akita, don't allow any argument. Make the nudge or push swift and decisive. Your remarks should be crisp and final. Don't debate the issue; stay in command of the situation, regardless of the dog's response to your corrective actions. Then, immediately change the subject. Don't dwell on the error committed. Lead the dog to the yard and begin some new play or training exercise.

Caring for Your Akita

Grooming and caring for your Akita is an important part of its bonding and training.

Teeth and Their Care

Puppy Teeth

Puppies are born toothless. Canines, like humans, have two sets of teeth: deciduous (temporary or milk teeth), and permanents. The first deciduous teeth to erupt are the incisors in the front of the mouth. Those 12 teeth begin to peek through the gums at four to five weeks of age. There are three of them on each side, six on the top and six on the bottom.

Dogs have four baby canine teeth, one on either side, top and bottom, just behind the third incisor. They erupt at about the same time as the incisors.

The 12 premolars erupt about a week later, and are positioned behind the canines, three on each side, top and bottom. They complete the set of 28 deciduous or milk teeth.

At about 12 weeks of age, the central deciduous incisors begin to loosen and are quickly replaced by permanent teeth. Usually by 16 to 20 weeks of age, all 12 permanent incisors are in place.

The four permanent canine teeth are often the last to appear, and typically are not visible until about six months of age.

Permanent premolars begin to erupt at about 16 weeks of age. There are four on each side, top and bottom, and the rearmost is usually visible by six months of age. Those 16 permanent teeth take the place of the 12 deciduous premolars.

The two upper molars on each side and three lower molars on each side also begin to appear at about 16 weeks, with the last of the ten erupting at about six months.

Adult Teeth

Check your Akita's teeth periodically. You may be amazed to find that at about six to seven months of age, Koby has two sets of canine teeth. It is not uncommon for a dog's permanent teeth to emerge from the gums before the deciduous teeth have shed out. If the baby teeth are loose and wriggly, don't worry about them.

To ensure a handsome smile and sweet breath, clean your adult Akita's teeth regularly.

However, if the permanent teeth have reached full growth and the baby teeth are still visible, the deciduous teeth might need extraction. Don't attempt this at home; a pair of pliers will just break them off, and you will still have the expense of a trip to the animal hospital. If the baby teeth are not removed, they may interfere with the placement of the adult teeth, but probably they won't. The significance of double teeth is that the tight space between them collects hair and debris, contributing to halitosis and gum infection.

If you give your dog rawhide or nylon bones to chew, and it is fed basically on dry dog food, its teeth should not require much routine care. Dogs rarely develop cavities unless the teeth are broken. Older dogs, and dogs that don't chew a lot, may be subject to dental tartar deposits. As the plaque builds up, it invades and erodes the gums and causes bacterial infections (gingivitis) to begin. If allowed to progress unchecked, gingivitis will eventually cause the teeth to loosen. Chronic gum infection may predispose older dogs to arthritis, heart disease, and kidney disease.

Cleaning Your Dog's Teeth

To prevent such dental problems, examine your adult Akita's teeth every few months. If you see yellow tartar, try cleaning the teeth with gauze pads moistened with hydrogen peroxide. The peroxide will help control gingivitis, and often will dissolve the soft, early dental tartar.

Canine toothpaste and toothbrushes are available from your veterinarian or from pet supply stores. Most dogs don't like to have their teeth brushed, but when compared to the alternatives, brushing isn't a bad program. If tartar is allowed to build, your veterinarian can scale the teeth with ultrasonic equipment and dental

instruments. Sometimes that procedure requires a short-acting general anesthetic and can be expensive.

Ear Care

Ear cleaning is rarely much of a chore in erect-eared breeds like Akitas. If you notice a significant amount of wax or dirt in the outer ear canal, it is easily cleaned with a cotton ball moistened with alcohol. Never pour any cleaning solution into the ears unless advised to do so by your veterinarian. If your dog scratches at either or both ears continuously, or holds its head tipped to the side, have the ears examined before initiating any treatment.

Calluses

If your Akita spends most of its time on a lawn, it isn't likely that calluses will develop. If kenneled on wooden or concrete floors, however, calluses may form at the points of contact with the hard floors. Calluses are unsightly, but they aren't generally a serious health problem unless they become infected. They are usually first seen on the outside of the animals' elbows; later they may form on the hocks, sides of the feet, and on the hip bones.

Maintenance care for dogs that are kept on hard surfaces should include lanolin and vitamin E applications to callus formations to keep them soft and pliable. Hard, cracked, and infected calluses may be of great concern in your Akita after the age of six or seven.

Boarding

If you need to board your Akita, check with the breeder who raised your puppy. Sometimes breeders have the facilities to keep outside dogs for a time. If possible, avoid boarding your Akita in a commercial kennel, as kennels present stress-related health risks to the dogs boarded there. Family pets resent being enclosed in small areas. Some become bored with inactivity; others are frightened or challenged by the commotion and barking of their kennel mates. Diet changes add to the stress of kenneled dogs. The odors of females in season are unnerving to intact males.

Of course, some boarding kennels are spotless and well managed, but unfortunately, not all. They may be a source of fleas, ticks, lice, and other external parasites. Although less likely, inadequate cleaning may also predispose boarders to intestinal parasite infestation. The most common complaint resulting from boarding dogs is *kennel cough*. This chronic, deep, croupy, honking cough may persist for weeks after the pet returns home.

If boarding your dog in a commercial kennel can't be avoided, visit the boarding facility before you need it, and ask to tour the kennel. If a tour is denied, you are in the wrong kennel. If you are allowed to walk through the boarding facility, watch for sick animals—signs of diarrhea, vomiting, coughing, and sneezing.

If possible, locate a kennel that specializes in boarding large dogs, one where each dog has its own private indoor space connected to an outdoor run. The best type of facility will have outdoor runs that are separated by block or brick walls instead of wire fencing. Such an arrangement will minimize conflict with neighbor dogs, and will also reduce the probability of exposure to respiratory infections.

Dogsitters

If you have constructed a kennel run in your yard, or if Koby is a trusted house dog, find a neighbor or friend who will care for Koby in your home. That person should naturally be introduced to him as frequently as possible before he or she takes on the responsibility of your pet's care. Don't forget that Akitas characteristically will allow friends into their homes when their owners are present, but when alone, they go on autopilot guard duty. Invite your friend to your home to feed Koby for several days while you are present in the background. Then perhaps repeat that drill once or twice while you stay away from the house altogether. Eventually, Koby should become used to his "dogsitter."

Veterinary Care

An annual maintenance trip to your veterinarian is strongly advised, even if your Akita is in perfect health. New animal health ideas and products are introduced frequently in veterinary medicine. Research information may reveal better ways of immunizing dogs, treating or controlling parasites, preventing heart worm infestations, or detecting diseases.

A quick physical examination is easily combined with the annual vaccinations that your dog requires. Your animal doctor's trained eyes and hands may discover minor problems that can be corrected before they become serious. That annual visit is an excellent time to discuss diet supplements, skin and dental care, or aging problems such as calluses, cataracts, and heart conditions.

Spaying

This procedure is critically important for female pets. Various contraceptive procedures don't take the place of ovariohysterectomy (spaying). Injections or oral tablets to prevent estrus, plastic diapers, and intravaginal devices intended to prevent breeding are available, but they are sometimes dangerous and aren't a substitute for spaying.

Ovariohysterectomy refers to the total surgical removal of both ovaries

An Akita and his boy.

When spayed at six months of age, mammary tumors and other reproductive hormone-related diseases are avoided for life. All female pet Akitas should be spayed before their first heat period.

Early Spaying
There is a strong movement in the dog shelters of the United States at the present time to spay dogs and cats at three months of age or less. It is intended to control reproduction, reduce the strays, and minimize the number of animals that are euthanized in shelters. This technique has been well researched, and is performed on pets before adoption. It may be another way that breeders can assure that pet-quality puppies are not inadvertently bred. The procedure is quite safe and predictable, and causes few side effects.

Risks of Spaying Later
In case you don't have your Akita female spayed at six months old, the surgery is still a viable option at a later time. Age constitutes only a minor risk in strong and healthy females up to four or five years. After that age, each year brings with it new risks to be addressed:
• Abdominal surgery involving obese animals presents higher risks than when performed on young, lean, athletic dogs.
• Anesthesia may also be complicated in fat dogs.
• Longer incisions are necessary to accommodate the fatty structures being removed.
• Sutures do not hold as well in fatty tissues, and healing time is often prolonged.

Spaying and Obesity
All spayed or neutered dogs get fat, right? Wrong! *Dogs are fat because their dietary intake exceeds their caloric needs.* There are many reasons for

and the uterus. It is probably the most frequently performed surgical operation in small animal veterinary practices, and is one of the safest and most predictable. The time-honored optimum age to spay a pet is about five or six months, shortly before her first heat. Surgical risk is minimal at that age, the operation is easy to perform, and usually the cost of surgery is the lowest.

obesity, including hormonal imbalances, gluttony, lack of exercise, and hereditary predisposition. Rich foods, overfeeding, table scraps, and treats all contribute to obesity. There may be an association between spaying and obesity, but it is not a simple cause-and-effect relationship. There is no more excuse for obesity in normal spayed females than in normal intact females.

Spaying a female prevents or removes stresses that are related to the reproductive cycle. With those energy-demanding stresses removed, a spayed female requires fewer calories than before surgery. If her caloric intake is not adjusted to accommodate her reduced requirements, obesity will result.

It is a myth that spaying or neutering a dog causes obesity.

Castration

Young adult males that show aggressive tendencies may benefit from being neutered. The operation entails surgical removal of both testicles, altering the hormone balance within the dog. This safe operation changes his ideas about mating, and often reduces his propensity to mark his territory. There is no reason why castration should change a male's property-guarding instincts or his personality, and the surgery should not reduce his value as a family companion.

Castration precludes the possibility of testicular tumors, and virtually prevents prostate cancer and perineal hernia formation.

If castration is considered, it is usually done at eight to ten months of age, but there may be exceptions in aggressive dogs. The anesthetic and surgical risks are minimal, and recovery is nearly always quick and uneventful.

HOW-TO:
Grooming Your Akita

Bathing an Akita is sometimes an all day affair.

One of the first things the pup should learn is to stand still while you groom and pet it. Grooming equipment required to use on your Akita is minimal, but maximum patience is necessary. Only bathe your Akita if its coat is deeply soiled or fouled, or just before a dog show. Sometimes a bath will also help finalize the semiannual seasonal shedding. Pick a warm day, or plan to spend several hours in the house with your Akita. Have the following equipment available:
• stainless steel comb with wide-set teeth
• spray bottle of plain water
• metal pin brush
• scissors-type nail trimmer (Miller's Forge)
• styptic shaving stick
• electric hair dryer with warm setting
• bathtub (with hair-collecting drain stopper if you bathe the dog in the house)

• sprayer hose connected to a faucet
• mild dog shampoo without insecticides
• stack of dry towels
• cotton balls
• rubbing alcohol

Comb and Brush
Take your time combing and brushing all loose hair from the coat. This procedure may require several daily sessions. Don't forget to reward Koby

Brushing your Akita is part of regular maintenance.

when he stands patiently, and don't be too cross if he is impatient and anxious for you to finish. You will find it easier to control the Akita undercoat if you spray it with water before brushing and combing. Use a fine mist, and dampen the coat lightly. This will keep the soft hair from flying into the air, up your nose, and in your eyes.

Bathing
Place Koby in the bathtub and soak his coat thoroughly with warm water, holding the spray nozzle close to the skin. Use the shampoo sparingly and work up a lather. Keep the soap well away from his eyes, and don't squirt water into his ears. When you are satisfied that the entire coat has been lathered, rinse it out with the spray nozzle, going over the coat several times, until all shampoo is gone.

Towel Koby several times, rubbing the coat vigorously and changing towels frequently, to squeeze as much water as possible from the coat. Take him

58

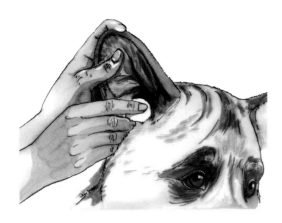

Clean the ears with cotton balls.

out of the bathtub and using the warm setting on the dryer, complete the drying procedure. Continuously brushing the coat under the dryer will hasten the drying process. Have patience; the Akita coat is absorbent, and takes a long time to dry.

Maintenance coat care consists only of periodic light brushing.

Nails

Trim the nails, using a sharp nail trimmer of the scissors type. Never use a dull instrument. Long, pointed puppy nails often need attention at two- or three-week intervals, but active outdoor Akitas may never require the nails of their forefeet to be trimmed from the time they are six months old until they are seniors. Hind nails get less wear, since they aren't used in digging, and they often need your attention on a regular basis. Nail trimming is not difficult, but sometimes restraint requires two sets of hands and a firm conviction on the owner's part.

If your Akita has a white toenail, begin with that one. The white nail is usually sufficiently transparent to see the blood vessels forming a point in the core of the nail. Your cut should be just beyond that forward-pointing, V-shaped vascular structure. By visually measuring the length of the white nail after trimming, you

should have a good idea about how much to take off the dark, pigmented nails.

If in doubt, begin cutting off thin serial slices of the nail, starting at the tip. As you progress, you will discover that the nail becomes softer with each slice. Near the tip of the nails, the cross sections of the slices will be hollow at the bottom; rather A-shaped. As you near the blood vessels, the slices will become more nearly circular when viewed in cross-sections.

Slight bleeding isn't what we hoped for, but if it happens, don't panic! The bleeding isn't likely to be profuse, but it will be persistent. A few drops of blood looks like a quart when spread over a white tile floor. To stop the bleeding, press a dampened styptic shaving stick firmly to the bleeding nail, holding it in place for several minutes.

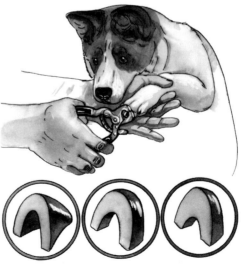

Proper equipment and great care are needed to trim black nails.

Akita Activities

Exercise

Akitas thrive on regular exercise; they are working dogs, athletes, and can become couch potatoes easily if allowed to do so. Exercise tends to keep puppies out of mischief, and produces solid musculature in growing youths. It keeps adult pets in prime condition and tends to minimize the effects of aging conditions such as arthritis. Obesity can be combated through an exercise and diet program.

If you are fortunate in having a large yard, your Akita will no doubt initiate and play some games by itself, but laziness might also rear its ugly head. It's best not to rely on the dog's self-imposed exercise programs.

Begin informal obedience training early.

When children of the family are available to romp and wrestle with their Akita friends, exercise is rarely a problem. However, if the dog is kept indoors or in a kennel run, you, the owner are obliged to see to its exercise. Play sessions or long walks will supply the needs of your pet, providing they are regularly and frequently implemented.

If your lifestyle doesn't allow spending exercise time with your companion, you should consider a much smaller, more sedentary pet. When you assume the responsibility of Akita ownership, you accept the obligations that accompany that relationship, including exercise.

Formal Instruction

Formal obedience trial rules and regulations are available from the AKC. Local specialty clubs and all-breed clubs often sponsor obedience trials, matches, and training classes, and excellent obedience instruction is offered by some of the pet supermarkets. Attend these classes with your dog, and you will benefit tremendously from the instructions offered. Remember, instructors will teach you how to train your dog—they won't train him for you!

Obedience training will help you fine-tune your Akita's manners. Instructors will help you learn how to control your pet in the presence of strangers, both humans and dogs. The various obedience exercises will sharpen your ability to communicate with your dog, and will illustrate the right way to handle your Akita in many different circumstances.

If you aren't interested in entering your Akita in formal trials, the training is still beneficial, and even the class dropouts come away from a well-managed obedience class with better manners than they had before.

When to begin: Obedience classes can be started when your dog is about four months old, and all Akitas will benefit from that early training. If a professional is hired to train your dog, make sure that he or she uses only positive reinforcement with your dog. Walk through the training with the trainer. Many shortcuts, using negative means, can be used with submissive breeds, but they absolutely won't work with Akitas. There is no place for punishment in training any dog, but it should particularly be avoided in an Akita. A trainer who bullies your dog can spoil it for life.

Canine Good Citizen Tests

Dog clubs throughout the United States administer good citizen tests for dogs. This program, promoting good manners and behavior, is sponsored by the AKC. Owners have their dogs evaluated for ten different activities that help to assure that their dogs are good neighbors. There are no points involved; the scoring is a simple pass or fail evaluation. These essential, easily taught activities include allowing a stranger to approach, walking naturally on a loose lead, walking through a crowd, sitting for examination, reacting to a strange dog, and reacting to a distraction such as a door suddenly closing or a jogger running by the dog.

Good citizen evaluations are made by AKC member clubs, and information about them may be obtained by contacting the AKC or an all-breed club in your community. Having a Canine Good Citizen Certificate hanging on the wall is evidence that your Akita has been trained. It means that you love your dog enough to spend the time training it, and that Koby is a good neighbor.

Weight Pulling, Skijoring, and Sledding

If obedience trials aren't particularly interesting to you, your working dog may be engaged in other endeavors. Perhaps you live in a part of the world where there is significant snowfall. Check with local dog clubs to see if any sponsor weight-pulling contests. If so, your adult Akita can be a competitor with a minimum of training. Pulling dogs must be fully mature, and are divided and classed according to their body weight. Your Akita has the strength and power to participate if you have the time to train it.

Dogs are fitted with specially constructed harnesses and hitched to sledges loaded with dead weight. Upon command the sledge is jiggled to break it loose from the snow, and the dog is encouraged to pull the loaded sledge a designated distance in a specific amount of time. These contests are great fun for the participants and the owners alike. The tremendous heart of the Akita makes it particularly adaptable to these power endeavors.

Skijoring is an exciting sport.

Some components of an agility obstacle course.

Skijoring is an equally fun and exciting sport that provides exercise for your dog and many thrills for you. Koby is fitted with a sledding harness, and you are fitted with skis. The rope extending from his harness is held like a waterskiing towline. The rest is up to your imagination. Sometimes, to add speed and excitement to the sport, more than one Akita is used. It's best to have a wide open, snow-covered field when you begin this sport, as trees have a way of creating hazards for the skijoring team, both the dog and the driver.

Sled teams made up of two Akitas provide yet another winter sport that can furnish exercise and training for your dog. Akitas make good sled dogs, individually or in pairs, but they are usually too aggressive to be harnessed in teams made up of other breeds of dogs.

Agility

Agility contests were only recently introduced to the United States, but various countries in Europe have held them for many years. Competition in agility requires extensive training and active participation by the owners. As in obedience trials, agility dogs must work off lead, in the presence of other dogs and their owners. Akitas must be carefully evaluated and conscientiously chosen for agility trials. Only those that are less aggressive, and raised in the presence of other dogs are likely to be of the proper temperament to do well in these contests. If your Akita is from a line that has been shown in obedience trials, and is easily trained and responsive under all circumstances, it might do well.

The AKC designates Novice, Open, and Excellent classes, and awards titles accordingly. There are tunnels to run through, obstacles to leap over, teetering bridges to cross, and planks to walk. The owners walk or run alongside the dogs, encouraging them. If your Akita can be trusted off

lead, it is a wonderful participation sport to pursue. It involves agility, training, athletic ability, and trust.

Dog Showing

Another activity for your Akita is the show ring. Showing a dog, especially an Akita, can be a rewarding experience. Here is a breed that, aside from a bath before the show, requires virtually no grooming, no artificial makeup, and no scissoring or clipping. The only preparation needed is training your Akita to behave itself in the presence of strangers. It must tolerate having the judge check its teeth, and handle it from stem to stern.

Show training should begin as a puppy, and your Akita must work well on leash. It helps to teach it to "stack" each time it stops, but that pose is almost natural to an Akita. In a dog show, the competitors are judged in a standing position that displays the dog to the best possible advantage, so that the judge sees only the finest conformation the dog has to offer. That is called *stacking*.

Show dogs don't come already programmed to behave on leash and to answer commands. It takes a tremendous amount of patience attending classes and learning to train your Akita. Dog shows involve time and expense and significant traveling.

You mean that I'm supposed to go in there?

HOW-TO:
Entertaining Your Akita

Playing Ball

Games Akitas play include many of their own making, as well as those we teach them. Few will play ball; it seems to be beneath their dignity to repeatedly chase an inanimate object and retrieve it time and again. If Koby is not a ball player, sometimes a soft Frisbee or an empty two-liter plastic soda bottle will create more interest. Remove the cap and paper label from the bottle before you give it to the dog.

Sometimes the game is one-sided, with Koby keeping the Frisbee or bottle away from you most of the time, while you are always trying to retrieve it. As you might have guessed, he doesn't always want to bring the bottle to you obediently each time it is thrown. Oh well, you probably need exercise too.

Frisbee playing is fun.

Be sure to remove labels and tops from pop bottle toys.

Hide-and-Seek

The Akita's natural posses-siveness of toys can be used to your advantage in the game of hide-and-seek. If Koby has a favorite toy, have another member of the family hold him while you hide the toy in some obvi-ous place in the yard. Then turn him loose and watch him scram-ble to find the hiding place. Choose less and less obvious hiding places as Koby becomes more adept at sniffing out the toy. When the game is over, give the toy to Koby to put away.

Sniffing Out Objects

Hide-and-seek can be expanded to include sniffing out hidden objects of all kinds. It can be played indoors, and is a fine way to get your Akita up and into action.

Choose some treat such as a piece of jerky. Let Koby smell the jerky, then shut him in another room. Hide the jerky under a table or around the cor-ner in the kitchen. As Koby gets the idea, make the game harder by putting it under a rug, behind a couch, or other place where it must be sniffed out.

Progress from the jerky to an object that is not so tasty—a piece of clothing that you have worn, such as a sock, serves quite well. Again, let Koby smell the sock, then shut the door and hide it under a pillow or some such place where it can be found only by using his scenting ability.

This idea may be expanded to tracking lessons, wherein dogs are taught to track a human scent over a given course. Although Akitas aren't often found in AKC tracking contests, their heritage in hunt-ing makes them viable candi-dates for the exercise. If you are lucky enough to have an Akita with a special nose for the sport, follow it up.

Roadwork

Walking is more fun when accompanied by your Akita, but first, Koby must accept the leash and be trustworthy when it is in place. With a chain collar and a strong leash on your companion, find a trail that is smooth, soft, and shady. If you

Hide and seek is a fun game for Akitas.

64

Both of you need exercise.

walk in the early morning or late evening, both you and he will enjoy the exercise more. You will meet other walkers frequently, some with dogs, so it is important to maintain control of Koby at all times. Always keep him on a short, loose leash when using public trails. If it is warm weather, carry a bottle of water for yourself and Koby.

Heavier roadwork, such as jogging or running on tracks, or the sidewalks of your neighborhood are fine exercise for your adult dog. Don't subject a puppy to heavy roadwork. After about 18 months of age, Koby's bones and joints will be sufficiently mature to withstand the shock produced by roadwork on pavement or concrete.

It's tempting to take Koby for a spin beside your bike. Don't do it! An Akita is strong enough to pull your bicycle over when you least expect it, or Koby may take off after a cat, trip on his leash, and before you can react, become

Akitas are well suited to back packing.

tangled up in your bike spokes and suffer serious damage to his feet and legs—and you!

Sometimes a shady country lane seems so deserted that you are inclined to let Koby run alongside your car. Suppress the thought! If you try to exercise your buddy without leaving your car seat, you will have trouble: You will meet another car, or some fool exercising an Akita on a bicycle, and the resultant tangle will take hours to sort out. It is dangerous to try to exercise your dog while saving your own strength. Give it up; it isn't worth the effort no matter how isolated you think the road is.

Backpacking
Hiking trips and backpacking on weekends is a sport that both you and Koby can enjoy. Buy a backpack that is well fitted to your dog. Puppies over six months old can carry an empty pack. As Koby matures, gradually load his pack. At a year of age, he can probably carry his own food, but be sure to load the pack evenly and start out with short trips into the woods. Once accustomed to the pack, a mature dog should be able to carry some of your provisions as well. Don't overload him! Use your head, and stop frequently for rest periods.

Nutrition

This discussion is general, and applies to maintenance diets. Specific comments on reproductive, neonatal, and weaning nutrition are found in other sections of this book. It is beyond the scope of a pet owner's handbook to discuss the interplay of vitamins, enzymes, trace minerals, and other nutritional elements. Instead, there follows a comprehensive, hands-on discussion about feeding your Akita.

Components of a Good Diet

Proteins

Dogs need amino acids in proteins for growth. Amino acids (protein components) from vegetables have lower bioavailability than those from animal proteins. Dogs are carnivores, (meat eaters). Plant protein is of lower quality than animal protein, relative to canine optimum nutrition.

Fats

Adequate fat must be included in Akitas' diets. Fat is a calorie-dense nutrient, containing nine Kcal per gram. (One Kcal is the energy needed to raise one kilogram of water from 15°C to 16°C.) That is more than twice the calories of protein and carbohydrates. This is true of both animal fat and vegetable oil. Preferred taste (palatability) is the principal difference between vegetable oils and animal fats; both provide adequate fatty acids that are essential for metabolism.

Carbohydrates

Starches, or carbohydrates, are another source of calories derived from plants. They are important as principal sources of glucose in human diets, but they are not significant in canine nutrition. Although carbohydrates are not required by dogs, diets without them are impractical to produce commercially. Diets high in carbohydrates containing protein and fat that are also of plant origin are not recommended. The best nutrition for a dog is a food that combines animal protein with plant carbohydrates and fats.

Water

Water is essential for life. Plenty of fresh drinking water should be available at all times.

Commercial Dog Foods

All dog foods are not alike. If the package of dog food you are planning to buy doesn't plainly list its composition, pick another product. Dog foods containing the best ingredients and balanced nutritional elements will proudly display that information.

Read package labels; call or write to manufacturers. Know what you are feeding! To buy dog food based on price or total protein quantity makes no more sense than choosing a food by the picture on a box or bag. The sources and quality of protein, carbohydrate, and fat are as important as the quantities. Think of ingredient *quality* as well as quantity. Don't base your selection on a TV ad showing a beautiful litter of puppies or a happy companion dog. Those paid actors are marketing tools that may or may not be promoting a superior dog food.

Don't buy excessive quantities of dry dog food at one time. Storage takes its toll on nutrients; fats may become rancid; vitamins A, D, E, K, and some B complex may be lost. Beware of buying dry dog food from stores that have low product inventory turnover.

Preservatives and additives help maintain palatability of dry foods, and protects them from early oxidation. Some foods are preserved with natural antioxidants such as vitamin C and E, and contain no artificial preservatives. They are often the best. Don't store the food at high temperatures, because deterioration is enhanced by elevated temperatures.

Many premium foods are available in pet supply stores, supermarkets, and from veterinarians. Those products will provide desirable nutrition throughout the life of your Akita. Nutritional information on the package will specify whether the product provides optimum nutrients for growth in puppies, brood bitches, lactating dams, or adult maintenance.

Dog Food Labels

Some labels state that the food meets the recommendations of the National Research Council (NRC). That statement may apply only to canine maintenance requirements and should be adequate for pets under minimal stress. For growing puppies or breeding animals, maintenance foods aren't acceptable, and don't supply the increased energy demands of growth, pregnancy, or lactation.

Labels may specify the quantities of available nutrients, not the *bioavail-*

Don't choose a bargain brand dog food.

able nutrients (the amount that can actually be used by the dog for its energy requirements). If an essential element is fed to a dog in a form that is not bioavailable, it might as well be left on the store shelf.

Always look for the source of protein. The ingredient list should give you that information. Vegetable protein sources such as corn or soy flour may provide an excellent analysis on the package, but it may be misleading if the protein is not bioavailable.

Feeding Trials

You will find foods with label declarations that they have passed the American Association of Feed Control Officials (AAFCO) feeding trials for the entire life cycle of canines. You can generally rest assured that products so labeled contain the right amount of bioavailable food elements required for puppies, youths, and adults.

If the AAFCO declaration is not shown, get a phone number from the package and call the manufacturer to obtain feeding trial results. Ask about the source of protein and fat. Request

Plenty of fresh drinking water should always be available for your Akita puppies.

Semi-moist foods are palatable, but do not store as well. They are also expensive and contain some questionable chemical preservatives that are not found in dry foods.

Dry foods are usually the least expensive and easiest to feed. Most premium brands also pass the taste test and are well accepted by dogs.

Generally, premium dry dog foods contain adequate nutrition, require no supplementation, and are sufficiently tasty to suit most finicky appetites. In many cases, they may be fed free-choice, where the food is left out so the dog has access to it at all times, to be eaten whenever desired. Naturally, that is not an option if your Akita is a glutton.

To increase palatability, a basic diet of complete and balanced dry food can be mixed with canned food of the same type.

printed information about formulation of products, and whether the formula is kept constant, regardless of the seasonal variation of ingredient costs.

If you are unable to obtain the desired information about a product, choose another brand. If you are unable to understand the information provided by manufacturers, consult with your veterinarian or if he or she isn't able to help you make the decision, borrow a text on the subject. Most veterinary clinics have numerous reference sources for nutritional requirements of dogs.

Generic Brands

When shopping, always consider generic brands, but before buying, be sure they conform to the standards discussed here. Check the amounts and sources of essential elements, as well as AAFCO feeding trial results.

Types of Foods

Three types of dog foods are presently on the market; many companies produce all three.

Canned foods are expensive, but they store well and are highly palatable.

Supplements

It's poor economics to feed a bargain brand of dog food, hoping to cover its deficiencies with a cheap vitamin-mineral supplement. If a balanced diet is being fed, supplements are unnecessary; therefore, it is wise to check with your veterinarian before feeding a vitamin-mineral supplement to your Akita.

It's unnecessary to add raw meat, bone meal, or other similar products to your pet's already balanced diet. For many years, nutritionists recommended adding meat, especially liver, to dry dog food diets, but protein quality was suspect and amino acid deficiencies were sometimes experienced in those diets.

Contemporary research by pet food manufacturers, private research foundations, and universities, have unveiled more information about nutritional needs of our pets. Complete and balanced diets have been formulated for us. For those readers who want to delve into the intricacies of canine nutrition, we recommend a book entitled *Nutritional Requirements of Dogs, Revised*, from the National Research Council, telephone 1-800-624-6242. That volume is updated regularly, and will answer virtually all technical questions about canine nutrition.

Homemade Diets, Snacks, and Treats

Formulation of diets in the family kitchen often leads to problems. It's best to leave dog food production to those who have laboratories, research facilities, and feeding trials to prove their products. Rarely are dog owners able to formulate a balanced canine diet in their kitchen. If you feel that you must add to the packaged diet that is purchased for your Akita, try some commercially available treats. Liver flavored tidbits are acceptable, providing they aren't overused. Rawhide chew sticks and nylon bones are also excellent long lasting treats, and are good for the dog's teeth. Various flavors of hard, baked dog biscuits are available to add variety to the dog's diet. Although table scraps should generally be avoided, small bits of cooked meat may be fed as special treats on occasion.

Frequency of Feeding

Puppies should be fed free-choice dry food, plus two meals of canned and dry food (mixed) daily. This should be gradually increased as the puppy grows. The mixture should be about half dry and half canned food, and the amount of the mixture to be fed at each meal depends on the age and size of the puppy. Moist meals should constitute approximately half of the puppy's total dietary intake until six months of age. From six months until the puppy is a year old, the free-choice dry food is continued, and one moist meal per day is fed. The single

Posing for a portait is serious business.

moist meal that is fed after six months of age should approximate one fourth or less of the puppy's total dietary intake. At one year of age, most dogs will do quite nicely on free-choice dry food alone.

The exceptions to the rule include gluttonous eaters, or multiple dog households where other dogs are gluttonous eaters. Another exception is the dog with a finicky appetite, a condition rarely seen in Akitas. When it does occur, however, the meals of canned plus dry food may be continued.

If free-choice feeding is not a viable option for your home, feed puppies three times daily, dogs from six months on twice daily.

Breeding Your Akita

Pre-Breeding Evaluation

If your Akita is a superior example of the breed, and has proven herself in the show ring, you might decide to breed her. But, before you venture into that arena be sure you are mentally, financially, and physically able to assume the responsibility of breeding the dog. Ask an established Akita breeder to help you plot out a course of action before you commit yourself.

Akitas are popular dogs at this time. Their popularity has produced many amateur breeders that are filling the market with average and below-average dogs. Consider your own motivation: Is your primary motive for breeding your female to produce excellent quality puppies that have beautiful, trustworthy temperaments, or is it monetary? Hopefully, before you enter into a breeding program, you will think carefully.

If your motives are pure, and you decide to produce a litter from your female, draw up a plan and try to establish the probable markets for your pups. How many Akita puppies are presently being offered for sale in your area? Should you breed her now, or will it be better to wait six months?

Breed Faults

Prior to the mating, it is an excellent idea to have both breeding Akitas "faulted" by an experienced breeder or judge of the breed. Slight discrepancies from the breed standard are expected, since there is no such thing as a perfect Akita. If both sire and dam carry the same minor imperfections, their progeny may exhibit major faults.

The Veterinarian Check

When you have decided to breed your female, both she and the chosen sire should be physically examined, preferably by the same veterinarian, who should be furnished with breeding and health histories of both animals. Your veterinarian will also want to examine for, or see certifications of, normal hip conformation for both the male and female, as well as eye and other hereditary problems. Please note that the OFA hip certification is not done before two years of age. Because hereditary eye conditions are increasing in frequency in Akitas, special attention should also be given to these problems.

Physical Examinations

The female's reproductive tract can be examined without sedation. Visual examination of her vulva, vestibule, and vagina is usually accomplished using an endoscope.

A male's reproductive organs are more easily examined than a female's. Abnormalities of testicles and accessory structures are easily perceived by visual exam and palpation with practiced fingers.

Male dogs are born with their testicles positioned in their abdomens. By 30 days of age, both testicles should be descended into their scrotums. Testicle retention is hereditary, but the genetic mechanism is poorly understood. If retained testicles are not removed, they often develop malignant tumors.

Cryptorchids are males in whom neither testicle has decended normally

70

into the scrotum. Cryptorchids are typically sterile but not impotent. Dogs that have only one testicle descended into the scrotum are called *monorchids*. They are both virile and fertile, but since the trait is inherited, monorchid or cryptorchid dogs should be castrated before reaching puberty.

Vaccinations

Immunizations against contagious diseases are essential at the time your female is bred. Her immunity should be boosted to the maximum level so as to produce antibody-rich colostrum at the time of whelping.

Puberty

Akita puberty may occur at any time after about six months of age. Estrous cycles begin at puberty and occur on a regular schedule throughout a female's life until she is spayed. The best rule to follow when breeding your Akita female is to be sure she is mentally stable and physically mature. That is no earlier than her second or third heat period. Her hips cannot be OFA-certified until two years of age, hence the recommendation that she be at least two years old before breeding.

Phases of the Estrous Cycle

For a more complete discussion of reproduction, we refer you to *The Complete Book of Dog Breeding* by Dan Rice, *Barron's Educational Series, Inc.,* 1996.

Proestrus

Canine heat cycles are divided into four separate phases. The first phase of your Akita female's estrous cycle is called *proestrus*. A bloody vaginal discharge is produced, and she will usually spend an inordinate amount of time licking her external genitalia. The average length of proestrus is generally accepted to be nine days.

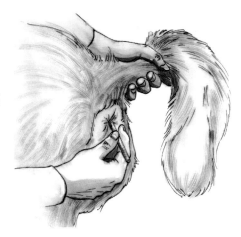

Her temperature drops just before she begins labor.

Estrus

The next phase of the reproductive cycle is called *estrus*. It averages nine days and it is during this period that a female can be bred.

Diestrus

The third phase is known as *diestrus*, and it lasts about 60 days and it is the period of pregnancy.

Anestrus

For about 100 to 150 days, a female's reproductive system is in a quiet stage of the estrous cycle known as *anestrus*.

Pregnancy

The terms *gestation* and *pregnancy* are interchangeable. Both refer to the physical and physiological state of females carrying their young. The terms *whelp*, *delivery*, and *parturition* all refer to the production of puppies at the termination of pregnancy.

The period of gestation extends from the time of successful mating to

Be sure to have your Akita examined by a veterinarian before you decide to breed him.

parturition. The average canine gestation is 63 days.

Nesting

During the last two weeks of pregnancy, you should consider confining your female to the particular area of the house that you plan for her to occupy during delivery and raising her puppies. That place can be any easily accessible room or part of a room. When she is not actually with the family, she should be kept in the special area.

A properly constructed whelping box.

Whelping

In canine breeding terminology, when a female delivers her puppies, the process is called *whelping*. Akita breeders need to be aware of the signs that accompany normal whelping, the stages of labor, and delivery itself (see below).

Don't subscribe to the concept and practice of taking over the dam's whelping responsibilities as, to do so will reduce natural, instinctive canine maternal behavior.

As an owner and breeder, you have the responsibility to only *oversee* your dog's whelping, and to render assistance when and if needed, but help should be reserved for those times when a puppy or the dam is at risk. Recognizing that your help is occasionally necessary, you must be aware of the elements of a normal delivery, be alerted to potential problems, and have the knowledge necessary to assist.

Body Temperature

Usually, the body temperature of a pregnant female drops from a normal of 101.5°F (38.5°C), to less than 100°F (38°C), often as low as 98 or 99°F (36.5 or 37°C). This happens about 12 to 24 hours before productive labor begins.

If you decide to take your Akita's temperature, it should be done three times a day, and to be a valid predictor, the temperature must be taken and recorded at the same times each day.

Imminent Whelping Signs

It is important to recognize the earliest signs of labor and parturition. Be aware that no outward signs are constant or predictable in all females.

Several days before labor begins, the pregnant female's appetite gradually diminishes. She becomes restless and sedentary.

Before breeding, both dam and sire should be examined for hereditary conditions common to Akitas, such as hip dysplasia and eye problems.

A sure sign that uterine labor contractions have begun is the presence of a green vaginal discharge that is the result of placental detachment from the uterus. That fluid may be seen several hours before the first pup is born. The thick green liquid, called *lochia*, is intermittently observed for a week or longer after whelping.

Labor

After her temperature drops and her appetite diminishes or ceases, your expectant Akita will begin acting strangely. She will pant, pace, whine, and dig at the floor of her nesting box, turn around several times, lie down, get up, and repeat the performance.

Finally, as whelping time approaches and the productive stage of labor begins, she lies on her side and begins to strain. A moderate quantity of clear, straw-colored or light pink fluid leaks from the birth canal.

If hard labor persists for four hours or more without the birth of a puppy, call your veterinarian immediately. Most deliveries are completed in four to six hours, but that time can vary.

Between deliveries, many dams wish to go outside. It's OK to allow her to go out for eliminations as often as necessary, *but only under close observation*. Unsupervised trips to the backyard may cause you to lose a puppy that was dropped in a snowbank or under a bush.

Delivery

Just before the first puppy emerges, an opaque bubble of placenta (amniotic sac) will protrude from the birth canal. The puppy's head and front feet are visible within the bubble. Then, with a final abdominal contraction, the puppy is forced from the birth canal.

The mother licks the puppy, rolling it over and over, cleaning all the blood, meconium (bowel contents), and placental debris from its body. While she is cleaning the puppy, she chews the umbilical cord in two, and frequently she consumes the placenta. It's far better to allow the female to eat all placental tissues than to interfere with her normal maternal instinct by taking them from her. The number of placentas produced should be counted if possible. If a small litter is whelped in a short period of time, that may be an option. In most whelping events that involve larger litters and take several hours, it isn't a practical undertaking. The bitch may produce and eat one or more afterbirths when the owner isn't present.

Dystocias (Difficult Births)

Dystocia is defined as any situation in which parturition does not begin, proceed, and conclude in a normal, progressive fashion. All dystocias must be treated as emergencies. Often the best assistance you can render your Akita in labor is to call your veterinarian for specific advice about an immediate problem.

When to Call for Help

As a rule of thumb, when serious abdominal contractions begin and placental membranes and fluid are seen, a puppy should be delivered within four hours. Typically, the time will be much shorter, but don't delay your call for help more than four hours.

If a puppy's nose is presented and visible at the vulva and no delivery progress is made for 10 or 15 minutes, call for help!

If black, thick, odorous fluid is seen before the first puppy is born, consult immediately with your veterinarian. The same is true if a thick, yellow, foul discharge is seen during the parturition process.

Green-colored fluids normally accompany parturition beginning a few minutes before the first puppy is delivered and lasting throughout the delivery process.

If your female seems depressed, disoriented, vomits (or attempts to vomit), acts weak, or staggers when walking, seek professional advice immediately.

Post-Whelping Problems

Hemorrhage

Whelping is messy, but most of the copious, light-colored fluids are obviously not whole blood. It is rare to see major hemorrhage at the time of parturition, but, if it is observed, it constitutes an emergency that requires immediate professional help.

Vomiting and Diarrhea

Vomiting immediately following whelping may be anticipated and is associated with eating placental tissues. Persistent vomiting, especially if the animal is weak, depressed, or uncoordinated, is cause for alarm. Take the dam's temperature, and if elevated above 102°F (39°C), call your veterinarian immediately. A feverish, disoriented post-parturient dam that is experiencing repeated vomiting needs immediate professional attention.

Puppy Care

Feeding the Lactating Female

If your Akita doesn't regularly leave her litter to eat, tempt her to do so by mixing her dry dog food with hot water, which will produce an aroma that should encourage her to eat. Make it more tasty by adding a bit of bland, low-fat beef broth or chicken broth, but don't suddenly begin supplementation with meats or rich foods.

If premium, energy-dense foods are fed year-round, the only dietary changes necessary are gradual increases in quantities fed. A dam's caloric energy needs are expected to be triple (sometimes quadruple) her pre-breeding maintenance requirements. When the puppies begin to eat solid food, decrease the dam's diet accordingly. Her caloric requirements diminish as her puppies begin to eat solid food.

Monitoring the Puppies

Puppy Activity

When whelping is finished, watch the puppies from a nearby vantage point. Notice their nursing habits, paying particular attention to individuals that differ from the rest. Watch for weak puppies, or ones that do not respond to their dam's attention.

After 15 or 20 minutes of observation from a distance, major differences between puppies should be obvious. Direct your particular attention to pups that act differently from the others, or ones that the dam pushes aside.

A puppy that is not allowed to nurse may have a physical or physiological deformity that requires your attention. To survive it must be examined, and possibly treated. If you can find nothing wrong with it, warm it up, and return it to the nest. If it is rejected repeatedly, call your veterinarian.

Puppy Examination

Akita puppies' eyelids are sealed shut at birth, and serious damage will be done to the eyes if you attempt to unseal them. Normally, the lids will begin to separate at about ten days of age. The ear canals are also sealed, and they open a day or two after the eyelids separate.

Puppies are born toothless, but you should examine the oral mucous membranes that cover the structures within the mouth. The gums, tongue, and lips should be moist and vibrant pink. Pale, gray, or blue-gray membranes are signs of serious problems.

Temperature

The normal puppy temperature at birth is about 97°F (37°C). It should increase gradually, reaching 101.5°F (38.5°C) by 21 days.

Don't overreact to hypothermic (low body temperature) pups! Infrared heat lamps or sun lamps will dehydrate and virtually broil puppies. If it is necessary to raise the nursery temperature, place a heating pad, turned on low, under one end of the nesting box bedding. Place a reliable thermometer on the puppies' bedding over the source of heat and monitor it closely. Keep it lower than 90°F (32°C).

Eating Habits

Normal newborn Akitas are usually found nursing or sleeping in a cluster.

Puppies' eyes and ears are sealed at birth.

If one is often found separated from its mother and siblings, examine it closely; there is probably a reason. Squeeze a drop or two of milk from a nipple and, while the milk drops are suspended on the tip, introduce the

By adulthood, your Akita's ears will be strongly erect and directed slightly forward.

nipple into the puppy's mouth and watch closely. It may have been shoved from a breast by a stronger puppy, and when it is allowed to nurse without competition, it will fill its stomach promptly. If it still refuses to eat, call your veterinarian.

If several of the brood are restless and crying and moving from nipple to nipple, the dam should be thoroughly examined. Take her temperature and check the milk supply from each gland. If her milk production is inadequate to meet puppy demand, review her diet, both quality and quantity, and have her examined by the veterinarian.

Colostrum

Virtually none of your Akita's immunity to infectious diseases is passed to her puppies before they are born; puppies acquire most of their protective immunity through the dam's colostrum (first milk). Colostrum is only produced for the first few days of lactation. It is a nutrient-dense milk that also contains high levels of antibodies.

Puppies that don't receive colostrum are at risk from infectious diseases and should be raised in a protected environment.

When Your Akita Moves Her Puppies

If the Akita dam isn't confined, don't be surprised if you hear puppies under your bed or behind the sofa. When you first see your Akita carrying a puppy, often she will have the pup's head inside her mouth, its body hanging limply from her jaws. Don't be alarmed—just direct her back to the "nursery" and confine her there.

Moving the pups is a sign that the dam is unhappy with their environment. Often the problem is associated with excessive human activity in the nursery, such as loud noises, children playing, people handling the puppies, or general confusion. Enforce a quiet rule, spend some time petting and reassuring her, and she will adapt.

Dewclaw Amputation

Dewclaws anatomically correspond to human thumbs. They are positioned on the inside of each foreleg, well above the origin of the other four toes. They don't touch the ground and are not used for walking or balance. About 15 to 20 percent of all Akitas have hind dew-claws that are attached more loosely to the legs. They are useless appendages that often snag on grass and weeds in the field. For those reasons, and for appearance, Akitas' hind dewclaws are usually amputated at three to six days of age by a veterinarian.

Make sure your nursing Akita gets all the nourishment she needs.

Weaning

At three or four weeks of age, most puppies are ready for supplemental feeding of semisolid food. A dry pre-mium puppy food is mixed with a small amount of canned premium puppy food. This mixture is then blended to gravy consistency with warm water, and will be accepted quickly by aggressive Akita puppies.

When all puppies have accepted the gravy, gradually decrease its water content, bringing the meals to the consistency of hamburger. Within a couple of weeks, they should all be eating three meals daily.

Some precocious Akita pups may begin to eat dry puppy food immedi-ately; others may not be interested for a week or two. By the time the litter is six weeks old, however, all should be eating solid food regularly.

Feeding the pups away from the dam is the first stage of weaning the litter, but don't enforce total separation from the dam or physically prevent them from nursing before six to eight weeks of age. She should be allowed to visit them anytime except when they are eating their solid food.

Weaning Age

Weaning puppies before they are emotionally ready can affect their per-sonalities. The only general rule is to choose a weaning age based upon

A litter of ambitious puppies.

the physical and mental maturity of individual puppies. Human bonding and the dam's attitude are equally important when deciding on the time for weaning. There is no particular magic age when all pups should be weaned. When a pup follows you away from its mother as you leave, it is fast approaching its weaning time.

Weaning Diet

As the puppies are separated from their dam, don't make any dietary changes except for increases in the quantities you feed them. To help discourage overindulgence of the heartiest eaters, and ensure that all get their equal shares, litters should be separated into groups of two or three when you are feeding them their moist meals.

Milk

Don't feed your puppies milk of any kind! Weaning is a stressful season in puppies' lives, and milk, rich foods, table scraps, and meat products are likely to cause diarrhea that adds to that stress.

A copy of the puppies' feeding schedule should accompany each puppy as it goes into a new home. Make sure the new owner realizes that dietary changes—other than gradual increases in quantities—can be dangerous and should be made carefully and gradually.

Socialization

Puppies must be socialized—and that doesn't happen overnight. The human bonding process begins shortly after their eyes open. As a conscientious Akita breeder you have an important obligation to handle your pups regularly during their first weeks of life.

Akita puppies probably require more intense socialization than other breeds. The time spent with them from two or three weeks of age until they are placed in their new homes is extremely important. This is the most vital period of an Akita's life for establishing a trusting relationship with humans. Early and extensive personal contact with your Akita puppies will make the difference between an average and a great pet.

Prospective Buyers

A word of caution is in order regarding prospective buyers. You will no doubt have friends and neighbors interested in your puppies. Akita breeders may wish to consider them as well, especially if your female is of superior quality. Other prospects will answer your advertisements.

Take great care when allowing people to handle your puppies before they are vaccinated. Some diseases, notably the upper respiratory varieties, are highly contagious and may be transmitted by human hands.

Many families have enough money to buy dogs, but no interest in caring for them. Ask questions about prospective owners' housing facilities and intentions. Be sure they understand the canine reproductive cycle and intend to have pets neutered at an appropriate age. Be especially wary of those who wish to purchase an Akita puppy as a gift or watchdog.

If possible, discuss these points with prospective buyers on the telephone before inviting them to see your puppies, and before actually offering them for sale.

Physical Exam and Vaccinations

At about six weeks of age, before they are offered for sale, puppies should be examined by your veterinarian, who will probably administer their first vaccinations also.

This examination will provide you with vital information about the individual puppies that should be passed on to their new owners. Their general health and any physical abnormalities that are discovered will be documented. Health and vaccination records will be furnished by your veterinarian at this time, as well as recommendations for future immunizations. Bring a composite stool sample from the puppies with you on this visit for microscopic examination for parasite larvae.

Care of the Dam's Coat

At about weaning time, when your lactating Akita dam loses patches of coat, don't overrespond. Adding coat supplements to a nursing female's diet may cause diarrhea, increasing the nutritional stress that led to the shedding.

The sticky, stringy, greenish vaginal discharge (lochia) persists for at least a week or two. This lochia will soil her bedding as well as her tail and hind legs. When the discharge has ceased, a bath may be in order, but remember that her puppies nurse a dozen times a day, and it isn't uncommon to find an aggressive pup trying to nurse its mother's ear or tail. Therefore, you

A puppy's vaccinations are critical.

should not expose the newborn puppies to shampoos containing chemicals that may be detrimental to their health.

Akita Health Care

When to Retire a Brood Bitch

If no health problems occur at an earlier time, Akita brood bitches should be retired by six or seven years of age. If breeding complications of any kind occurred, earlier retirement is prudent.

Although menopause does not occur in canines, the reproductive lives of females end much earlier than those of males. By five or six years of age, an Akita dam has usually passed her production peak, although she continues to cycle and exhibit normal heat periods. Problems related to whelping and puppies' health and size multiply with each passing year.

Metritis

Dystocias, combined with prolonged labor and decreased uterine tissue viability, seem to increase the probability of uterine infections. Metritis and pyometra are infectious diseases that occur more commonly in older intact females. They are sometimes fatal in young and middle-aged females, but their danger is multiplied many times in older animals.

Mammary Tumors

Breast tumors account for nearly half of all canine tumor cases, and at least half of those are malignant. They may occur at any age, but are more common in females past six years old. If spayed at or before puberty, the risk of mammary tumors is negligible, but each time she comes in heat, her predisposition for tumors increases.

The only viable therapy for mammary tumors is mastectomy, and often, several mammary glands are affected at once. A mastectomy is rarely done on a bitch of any age unless an ovariohysterectomy is performed at the same time. This radical surgery becomes more dangerous, and the prognosis becomes worse each year. Age is key—the older the bitch the more dangerous the surgery and the dimmer the prognosis.

Spaying Retired Females

Ultimately, the best advice for Akita owners is to retire your companion before serious maladies of age begin to show up. When the decision is made to retire her from reproductive or showing duties, schedule an ovariohysterectomy. Spay operations in older females are somewhat more difficult to perform, and there are slightly higher risks involved than in young animals, but those risks are minor compared to the risks of pyometra, tumors, and mammary cancer. *Ovariohysterectomy is the best insurance policy you can buy for your retired female Akita.*

Diseases Prevented by Vaccinations

As mentioned earlier, Akita vaccination schedules should be individually designed for adults and puppies. In neonatal pups, the breeder must consider colostral immunity, probability of exposure, puppy health, age, and stress.

Colostral antibodies have a limited life span and gradually diminish as the puppies mature. Live vaccines administered too early may not be effective because of existing colostral antibody levels. If administered too late, the window of opportunity for exposure to disease is enlarged. Timing is critical and should be discussed with your veterinarian.

The following discussion relates to diseases that are contagious and may be prevented by vaccinations at the appropriate time.

Canine Distemper (CD)

In spite of modern effective vaccines, canine distemper is still a significant threat to young puppies. Its mortality rate, lack of cure, and easy transmission make it an important canine disease. CD is primarily a neurological disease, but affected puppies may exhibit many symptoms including coughing, ocular and nasal discharge, pneumonia, inappetetence (lack of appetite), weight loss, weakness, staggering, diarrhea, and convulsions.

When contracted by young, unvaccinated pups, CD may cause sudden death. Other pups may seem to respond to various treatments, only to succumb to convulsions and paralysis at a later date. Even those that miraculously live through the disease are often scarred by hardened pads, tooth enamel deficiencies, and permanent neurological signs such as twitching of extremities.

The first of a series of CD vaccinations is given at about six weeks of age, and the product is usually combined with other vaccines. Annual boosters are required.

CAV-1

Infectious canine hepatitis is another highly contagious, incurable, fatal disease of dogs. Now known by the initials CAV-1 (canine adenovirus, type 1), it is a systemic disease that causes severe liver damage. Symptoms often mimic those of distemper and it may cause sudden death in young pups.

Where did everyone go?

Vaccines are highly effective in preventing CAV-1, and are usually combined with CD and leptospirosis preventive products. A series of vaccinations is begun at or after six weeks, with annual boosters.

Leptospirosis

This devastating kidney disease is sometimes fatal, and is caused by spirochete organisms. The disease is transmitted by urine from infected animals, and can affect humans as well as other animals. Treatment of a lepto infection may be effective, but permanent kidney damage resulting from an infection can be serious. Leptospirosis vaccine is usually combined with CD and CAV-1 immunizing products.

Parvovirus and Coronaviruses

Parvovirus and coronaviruses are among the more recently documented contagious, and often fatal, canine diseases. These diseases cause severe diarrhea, vomiting, dehydration, and depression, and they are especially devastating to puppies. Supportive therapy sometimes improves the prognosis, but in young animals, sudden death is common. Vaccinations are usually given at the same time as the other biologics, at or shortly after, six weeks of age, with annual boosters also required. Consult with your veterinary practitioner about the use of those injections.

Parainfluenza and Bordetella

A pair of respiratory conditions, caused by the parainfluenza virus and *bordetella* bacteria, cause coughing, fever, loss of appetite, and depression. They are highly contagious and are easily spread through the air. One cough or sneeze from an infected dog, and all dogs in the room are exposed. Unheeded, secondary pneumonia can result, and both conditions can be fatal.

These respiratory diseases typically have a lower fatality rate than some of the previously discussed diseases, but

they deserve serious consideration in your vaccination program.

Respiratory vaccines include intranasal types that are often less predictable than injectables, but their reliability is improving. Because of recent advances in vaccine research, consult with your local veterinarian.

Rabies

Vaccine for this fatal disease is usually administered at a later age than the others discussed. Many cities, towns, and counties have ordinances or laws that require rabies vaccinations to be administered when dogs reach three months of age, by or under the direction of licensed and USDA-accredited veterinarians. Those laws are made to address the public health significance of the disease.

Reservoirs for rabies infections are found in carnivores such as skunks, raccoons, coyotes, bats, and other wildlife. Since this incurable and fatal disease can be transmitted to humans and all other warm-blooded animals, great emphasis is placed on rabies preventive programs.

Other Common Diseases and Health Problems

Grass Awns

Whether your pet enjoys the freedom of a large yard or is temporarily confined to a dog run, be sure the areas are free from cheat-grass or wild oats. The seeds of those plants are attached to little beards that catch in your socks when you walk though them, and those same little bearded awns often make their way into dogs' ears, causing great discomfort and necessitating a trip to the veterinarian for removal. Some animals require sedation to accomplish that treatment.

Grass awns also may catch in the hair between your Akita's toes. If not discovered and removed promptly, the

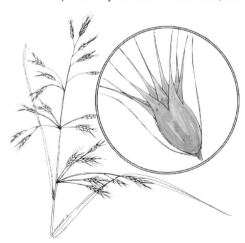

Cheat grass awns find their way into ears and feet.

sharply pointed little seeds penetrate the skin and begin to migrate into the tissue, requiring minor surgery to remove them.

Endoparasites

Intestinal parasites, especially roundworms, whipworms, hookworms, and coccidia may seriously affect the general health and vitality of puppies. Roundworm larvae may remain hidden in cysts in females' tissues throughout the dogs' lives. During pregnancy, larvae migrate from those cysts into the fetuses, and develop in the puppies' intestines, where they mature and produce eggs. Roundworm eggs in feces are the sources of infestation for other dogs (and possibly under certain rare circumstances, to children), and are found by microscopic examination of puppies' stools.

A stool sample from your dog should be taken to your veterinarian at least once a year. If parasite ova (eggs) are found in the stool sample, your veterinarian will prescribe an appropriate medication for treatment. Remember that worm medications are types of poisons. Be meticulous in calculating dosages and carefully administer the medication according to label directions.

An especially perilous procedure is to "worm" all puppies, whether or not a parasite infestation has been diagnosed. Discuss this with your veterinarian.

Heartworms

The microscopic heartworm larvae are picked up from an infected dog by mosquitoes. The larvae develop inside the mosquito, and are injected into another dog when the mosquito bites it. After further maturing, the adult heartworms, which have reached several inches in length and are the diameter of a piece of twine, are found living in the dog's heart. If only a few are present, there may be no outward signs, but if many are present, the ani-

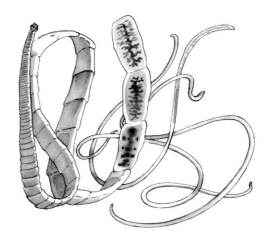

The tapeworm is a common parasite of dogs.

mal can show dynamic symptoms of heart failure. In either case, an infected dog acts as a reservoir of infection for other dogs.

The disease was originally found in warm, swampy areas of the country where mosquitoes prevailed, but in recent years, the disease has spread to nearly every part of the United States. Before a preventive program can be initiated, a blood test must show no larvae circulating in your dog's bloodstream. Prevention by means of oral medication is effective.

Skin Parasites

Dermatological problems such as fungus (ringworm) and mite infestations (mange) are often seen in weanling puppies. The most common mange mites are *Cheyletiella, Demodex, Psoroptes*, and *Sarcoptes*. Another mite, *Otodectes,* may parasitize ears of both cats and dogs.

As with other diseases, a definitive diagnosis must be made before treatment can begin. Skin scrapings examined under a microscope will identify the mites responsible for mange

Keeping your Akita's vaccinations up to date will keep your Akita healthy.

lesions. Examination of earwax will identify ear mites. Skin scrapings, ultraviolet light, or cultures are used to identify fungal infections.

Lice are seen occasionally in some areas of the country, and may be of the sucking or biting varieties. They are easily diagnosed and treated,

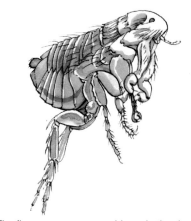

The flea causes many problems in the dog.

since all life stages live on the dog, and topical medication is usually satisfactory.

Don't rely on a universal mange dip or ringworm salve to cure skin diseases; those products may create new problems while doing nothing toward solving the initial one. Your veterinarian can suggest which treatments are most effective.

Fleas: These pesky parasites are common in backyard or kenneled dogs, and heaviest infestations are seen in the warmer climates. They live part of their life cycle off the dog, and are therefore more difficult to treat successfully than lice. Fleas act as secondary hosts for tapeworms, and fleas' saliva often causes an allergic dermatitis that is confusing to diagnose and difficult to treat.

Fleas are illusive. They bite, making a small wound, then lap up the blood as it oozes from the skin wound. Adult fleas have the ability to jump great distances, and they sometimes land on a human. They aren't terribly particular where they receive their meal. When a dog is around, the fleas will usually be found over the pelvic area or under the forelegs. One way to locate fleas is to use a fine-toothed comb and carefully run it through the coat over the pelvis. The fleas will be caught between the flea comb's teeth, or will jump from the hair in front of the comb. If the adult fleas aren't found, you may see some of their excreta (feces), appearing as tiny, black, comma-shaped debris.

Fleas, whether causing an allergy or not, are terribly irritating to the dog. They are often responsible for the animal licking, chewing, and scratching, and the formation of "hot spots," another serious skin condition.

If facing a flea problem, be aware that this parasite is a part-time resident of the dog. Once it arrives on its host, it feeds, mates, and lays eggs. The eggs are deposited on the dog, and fall off in the doghouse, on your carpet, or wherever the pet happens to be. The eggs hatch into larval forms that feed on dandruff and other organic debris in their environment. They pupate, and emerge to begin looking for a host. The adult flea can live for over 100 days without a blood meal.

If fleas are diagnosed, be sure to follow a long-term treatment program that uses products proven safe for the age of your dog.

There are now several new flea-repellent products available from your veterinarian. Some are in tablet form that are given orally, while others are in liquid form that is applied topically once a month. Some kill the flea eggs; others kill only the adult. Ask your veterinarian about the products, their safety, cost, and effectiveness.

New biological control schemes are presently being initiated in some areas. One involves the use of tiny nematodes that consume flea eggs, but won't affect humans or pets. Others involve the use of growth regulators that interfere with the flea's life cycle.

A new generation of flea collars are also available that repel the parasites rather than killing them after they have bitten the dog and caused their damage. There is a collar available that emits high-frequency sounds that is supposed to repel fleas, but its effectiveness is suspect.

Organic products such as pyrethrum and other "natural" insecticides are usually thought of as safer. That may or may not be the case, but they are much less effective than the contemporary methods.

Warning: Do not use oral medication, dips, sprays, powders, medicated collars, or other drugs that are not labeled for the specific age of your dog. Also, beware of all systemic medications in a pregnant or lactating female.

Going for a walk on a lovely spring day? Be sure to check your Akita for ticks when you get home.

Ticks: Adult ticks bury their heads in a dog's skin, and suck blood for days at a time. The males are tiny, about the size of a pinhead; the females often reach the size of a

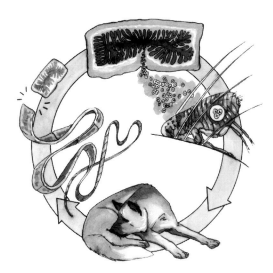

Fleas are the secondary hosts for tapeworms.

85

grape when they fill with blood. After a blood meal, they fall off, lay thousands of eggs, and die. Their other life stages may be completed on the dog (as in the brown dog tick), or they may use birds and other mammals for secondary hosts. They are often found under the collar, under the forelegs, around the ears, and over the withers.

The adult ticks that are found on your pet can be removed by grasping their bodies with a pair of tweezers or forceps, and with firm traction, pulling them out. After you have extracted the tick, clean the area with alcohol or another disinfectant daily, for several days. This will keep the scab off and allow drainage from the wound they have made.

A common belief is that ticks will be forced to detach if you heat their bodies with the flame of a match. It really doesn't make them back out any faster than pulling them. It is also occasionally advised that a drop of acetone, alcohol, or nail polish remover should be placed on the tick's body. Then you blow on it, and the rapid evaporation causes the tick to release its hold. That has more credibility, but it doesn't work every time. (Please don't try the alcohol, then a match; your dog might go up in flames!)

Ticks are responsible for several diseases in the dog. Tick paralysis is rarely seen, but may appear occasionally anywhere ticks are prevalent.

Lyme disease is spread by ticks. It is a treatable and usually curable condition, but may be fatal if treatment is inadequate or delayed. It doesn't occur in all regions of the country; your veterinarian has the latest information on its endemic areas. Biological preventive agents are presently being introduced to control Lyme disease, but the most reliable prevention is to control tick infestations. If your dog has an occasional tick and becomes ill, don't hesitate to take it to the veterinarian promptly.

Ehrlichiosis is another tick-borne disease to be reckoned with. It is transmitted by the brown dog tick, and is a serious disease, manifested by nose bleeds, swelling of the limbs, anemia, and a multitude of other signs. It can be fatal if not treated early and adequately.

Autoimmune Diseases

These diseases are characterized by the production of autoantibodies or white blood cells that attack molecules, cells, or tissues of the animal that produced them. The Akita seems to be a particularly good target for autoimmune diseases of various types.

Skin, coat, and fertility problems are often associated with hypothyroidism (decreased thyroid function) in the Akita.

Hypothyroidism: Perhaps the most important threat to the health of your adult Akita is hypothyroidism; with its various manifestations, it is the biggest single problem of the Akita. Although frequently diagnosed by lab tests, it is also empirically diagnosed by thyroid replacement therapy.

Hypothyroidism has an insidious onset, and most of the signs are related to a decreased metabolic rate. The affected dog will seek out warm places to rest, and will chill easily. There is a delay in reaction to stimuli, and the dogs become reluctant to take their usual walks. Symptoms of obesity, lethargy, and areas of hair loss follow. Affected animals lack their usual vitality and become listless. Females will fail to cycle normally, and fail to conceive.

VKH: Vogt-Koyanagi-Harada (VKH) syndrome is another autoimmune condition of the Akita that often accompanies hypothyroidism. It is assumed to be associated with the destruction of thyroid cells. Seepage of blood into the sclera, and a sanguineous discharge from the eyes is sometimes seen, together with loss of hair, skin lesions, and mouth sores.

Other autoimmune diseases include pemphigus foliaceus, which causes skin redness and deep crusts on the ears and foot pads, hemolytic anemia, and thrombocytopenia. The latter two diseases are related to blood and clotting deficiencies.

Eye Problems

Entropion, ectropion, microphthalmia, and progressive retinal atrophy are serious eye problems that are reported to be on the increase in the Akita.

Entropion refers to a turning under of the eyelids, an inversion of the lids, especially the lower ones. It can be surgically corrected, but is a hereditary problem, and should not be propagated in breeding stock.

Ectropion, another hereditary condition, is an opposite situation, and involves eyelids that are everted. It too may be corrected surgically in pets.

Microphthalmia is an abnormally small eye that isn't generally correctable.

Glaucoma and progressive retinal atrophy (PRA) are other congenital diseases sometimes reported in the Akita. Examination of breeding stock for these diseases is critically important. They can be treated, but cure is unlikely. An Akita affected with glaucoma or PRA may lose its vision, but that is not fatal. If the vision diminishes slowly, the dog will adapt and live a normal life span.

Gastric Torsion, Dilatation, and Bloat

One of the most devastating diseases of all large breeds of dogs is gastric torsion. There are many theories as to the cause of this often fatal condition. One practice that has been incriminated is feeding a single heavy meal, then water, before exercise. Another is feeding on the floor or ground, followed by activity.

Signs of the disease: About two to six hours after a meal, an affected dog suddenly begins to bloat, and its repeated attempts to vomit are ineffective. The dog has excessive salivation and quickly becomes toxic, staggers, and experiences intense abdominal pain. It has a tightly distended abdomen. Surgical intervention is mandatory, and not always effective. By the time it reaches a veterinary hospital, the animal may be suffering from advanced toxemia and heroic efforts to save the patient may be futile.

Preventive measures: There are a number of measures you can take to prevent gastric torsion:
• Feed your dog when activity is at a minimum.
• Elevate the dog's food bowl to minimize air swallowing.
• Encourage frequent, small meals, as with free-choice feeding.
• When you feed the major meal of the day, be sure that your Akita is quiet afterward.
• Don't allow the dog to engorge with water following a meal.
• Above all, curtail activity of the dog after any meal.

Canine Hip Dysplasia (CHD)

This controversial disease is a congenital condition that sometimes doesn't rear its ugly head until the dog is an adult. It is undoubtedly hereditary, but in a complex way. Parents that are OFA certified clear of the disease may still produce CHD puppies; in fact, it may crop up in puppies from bloodlines that are certified clear for several generations. The outward signs of CHD may not be apparent until the dog is mature, and begins to limp, and X-rays taken of a puppy's

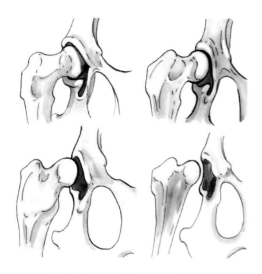

Hip dysplasia is a debilitating, hereditary disease.

The lovable Akita's expression.

hips are not conclusive. CHD predisposition is inherited and it is prevalent in certain bloodlines of all large breeds of dogs and some small ones. The Akita has no greater incidence of CHD than some other big breeds, but it is worthy of discussion.

In CHD, the head of the femur doesn't fit well into the acetabulum (hip socket) of the pelvis. It isn't deeply seated, and tends to rub in the wrong places, causing arthritis. CHD is a relative condition, and all dogs aren't equally affected. The appearance of lameness depends on the amount of displacement of the femoral head and the degree of damage to the cartilage that has been caused by the deformity. In most dogs, the disease shows up clinically by two or three years of age.

Signs of CHD are unilateral or bilateral hind leg lameness, difficulty in getting up from a lying or sitting position, and hind leg lameness when walking. It may progress to a point where the dog can't get up or walk. Those dogs are usually thin, and in pain most of the time.

Treatments include hip replacement, other surgical techniques to relieve pain, antiinflammatory drugs, and acupuncture. However, none of the treatments or medication will cure the disease, and only the prudent selection of breeding stock can prevent the condition from occurring.

Euthanasia

Putting a dog to sleep is a subject we all hate to discuss. It would be so convenient if our old dogs wouldn't suffer from their infirmities, and when their time is up, they would lie down and die. Unfortunately, it doesn't often happen that way. That's the reason for euthanasia—the final act of kindness, of stewardship. When administered properly, no dog suffers fear or apprehension. Your veterinarian will give your pet an injection, and it will be over in a few seconds.

A solid white Akita isn't uncommon.

With proper care (and a little luck), your Akita will age as gracefully as this senior citizen.

You can stay with your old Akita to the last, or go in the other room; that's up to you. If you are going to cry and fall apart, it's probably better to stay away. If you can hold the animal, giving assurance, it's better if you are there. In any case, euthanasia, in competent hands, may be better than watching your pet suffer and slowly die from an incurable illness.

Registration, Pedigrees, and Titles

Purebred Akitas may be registered by any of several canine registries in the United States, Great Britain, Canada, and Japan. Each has its own rules and policies. The American Kennel Club (AKC), registering about one million dogs a year since 1970, is the largest and probably oldest U.S. kennel club. Founded in 1884, AKC is a registration body, not a regulatory agency. It is a nonprofit organization dedicated to the welfare and advancement of purebred dogs.

The AKC does not license kennels or individual dog breeders, but does train and license dog show judges. The events that are held under AKC rules include conformation dog shows, obedience trials, agility contests, tracking tests, field trials, hunting trials, and herding trials.

Standards of all recognized breeds are maintained by the registry. The AKC registers 137 breeds that are separated into seven groups for the purpose of exhibition. Those groups include: Sporting, Hound, Working (which includes Akitas), Terrier, Toy, Non-sporting, and Herding. For the address of the American Kennel Club, see page 94.

Litter Registration

Data from various AKC documents were used for the following discussion. Other registries' policies and rules may vary, but the principles are the same.

When a litter is born, the owners of both sire and dam complete and sign a Litter Registration Application form that, together with an appropriate fee, is sent to the registry. When received, the AKC mails a litter kit to the dam's owner, which includes blue-colored, partially completed application forms for each puppy. One of those blue slips should accompany each puppy when it is sold.

The new owner completes the blue form, listing the sex of the pup, its color and markings, date purchased, and the owner's name and address. The puppy may also be named on the blue slip, and once a dog's name is registered, it can't be changed. The AKC invites complex names, so as to better identify each dog—simple names like Koby or Fido just won't do!

After the blue slip is completed and mailed to the registry with a fee, a permanent AKC Registration Certificate is printed and mailed to the new owner. Co-ownership or limited registration of purebred dogs is also possible.

Pedigrees

A pedigree is a genealogical document, a family tree that may contain three or four generations of a registered dog's ancestry. Pedigrees are often prepared by breeders on blank forms, or on computer formats. Those are not official documents in any sense of the word.

If an official AKC pedigree is desired, it can be purchased from the registry for a fee. Those documents list AKC exhibition titles as well as names and registration numbers for either three or four generations of the dog's ancestors. They can also be designed to show coat colors of those ancestors.

Titles

How many times have you heard someone say, "My neighbor has a grand champion thoroughbred Andalusian pitbull," or a "world champion South African alligator dog," or some other imaginative name and title?

Just for the record, there are a number of titles that are assigned to winners of competitive events sanctioned by the AKC. The AKC currently judges seven events. Of those, Akitas may compete in conformation, agility, and obedience but the methods of assigning the points and wins required to receive titles are beyond the scope of this book.

Conformation exhibitions or "dog shows" are designed to judge individuals of the same breed, and points are awarded for specific class wins, depending upon the number of competitors. Judges compare the animals with the breed standard that describes a perfect specimen of the breed, choosing or "putting up" the best of the class.

The title awarded to an animal that has proven its merit by earning sufficient points according to AKC rules is a Champion of Record. That title is abbreviated Ch. and is added as a prefix to a dog's AKC registered name.

There are three levels of obedience trial classes; awards made for those competitors that accumulate sufficient points are Companion Dog (CD) in the novice class, Companion Dog Excellent (CDX) in the open class, and Utility Dog (UD) and Utility Dog Excellent (UDE) in the utility class. Those titles become a suffix to the dog's name and are listed as such in registration and pedigrees.

Agility trials likewise award titles for Novice Agility Dog (NAD), Open Agility Dog (OAD), Agility Dog Excellent (ADE), and Master Agility Excellent (MAX).

Before venturing into purebred dog registration, or any of the various types of exhibitions, it is recommended that you acquire copies of information brochures and rule books from the AKC or whatever registry you plan to use. Registration and competition rules and regulations are not terribly complex but they differ from registry to registry, and compliance is critical.

Conformation Titles

All registered Akitas can be entered in a show, providing they are of minimal age, are physically normal and healthy, and have been trained sufficiently to behave in the ring. If they have any of the disqualifications listed in the breed standard they will be excused from the ring and barred from further competition. This is extremely important in the cases of aggressive breeds such as the Akita. They must always be trustworthy, since control is a vital part of participation in shows.

The Akita breed standard doesn't have any disqualification listed relative to temperament, but a hint that they require more training than the average dog is seen in the standard under Temperament (see page 16). It reads: "Alert and responsive, dignified and courageous . . . aggressive toward other dogs." That should immediately warn you that, to be exhibited, your Akita must be of a mild disposition, and trained well beyond the average. Aggressiveness is an extremely touchy point when competing in agility or obedience trials. There the dogs are worked off lead, and must be trustworthy around other dogs.

Doing a "figure 8" in a novice obedience trial.

Faults: Competitors are not allowed in the conformation show ring if they have any of the disqualifications listed in the standard. In the Akita, that includes males under 25 inches (63.5 cm) tall, and females under 23 inches (58.42 cm), incomplete nose pigmentation, drop ears, noticeably undershot or overshot jaws, and sickle or

Akitas in conformation competition.

uncurled tail. Females must be not be spayed, and the males must have both testicles normally descended into the scrotum. A conformation show is a beauty contest wherein a dog's conformation and movement are judged against the standard for the breed.

To do well and win in the contests, your dog should have a minimum of faults and be an outstanding example of the breed. You may elect to show the dog yourself or hire a professional handler. Be sure the handler is familiar with Akitas' temperament before you contract with him or her. Have your dog informally judged by an Akita breeder, and all of its faults outlined, then make the decision.

Classes: If it appears that your dog is of the quality to win, enroll it in classes. Many specialty clubs and all-breed dog clubs will have regular conformation classes. Enter the dog in fun matches for experience (yours and your dog's). If all goes well in the classes and matches, you are ready for the big time.

Winning: The AKC is particular about entries. Everything must be in order with the dog's registration, and the application must be correctly filed and mailed in by a deadline date. Your dog will compete against other Akitas of the same sex. The winner is awarded up to five points for each win, depending on how many dogs were entered in the show. After accumulating 15 points, under three separate judges, including two major wins of at least three points, your Akita earns the title of Champion of Record.

Although winning the prestigious title is a rewarding experience, a feeling of accomplishment will come with each near miss. Each time Koby competes, you learn something about the Akita, and he learns from you. To have a dog that glides along in the ring and receives the attention of the bystanders gives you a feeling of pride. To show well is an accomplishment in itself. To win is ecstasy.

Conformation shows are not judged on the basis of the breed standard alone. Judges have the responsibility to consider the dog's attitude and conditioning. Training and willingness are important parts of showing, and a dog that is enjoying itself exhibits better than one that is only going through the motions.

Obedience Titles

Novice obedience trials leading to the CD (Companion Dog) degree consist of:
- heeling on leash
- standing for examination
- heeling free
- recall
- long sit
- long down

Your Akita must be at least six months old before it can be exhibited, but these exercises should be mastered at home and in training sessions with other dogs before tackling an obedience trial.

Most clubs that sponsor obedience trials provide ample training exposure to ready your dog for a trial. Matches sanctioned by the AKC are another means of preparing for a trial. All the rules that apply to an AKC trial are employed at a sanctioned match, but they are more relaxed, and the pressure isn't as great as in a licensed trial.

As previously discussed, after your novice dog has earned sufficient points under three separate judges it will be awarded a CD degree. Then it is free to progress to the more advanced CDX (Companion Dog Excellent), UD (Utility Dog), and OTCH (Obedience Trial Championship). Each of these contests has higher standards and

Koby, down. Koby, stay. Good dog!

more difficult exercises, and only the best-trained dogs arrive at the UD or the OTCH degree.

Another obedience degree is TD (Tracking Dog), which is awarded to dogs that have successfully exhibited in tracking contests. When it is earned by a dog that already has a UD, it then earns the UDT (Utility Dog Tracking) degree, a highly coveted accomplishment. Some Akitas have the background to perform well in these obedience exercises if they have the temperament for the work. Their heritage includes scent training as well as general obedience work.

Obedience trials, agility trials, and conformation shows aren't for everyone. Just owning, training, enjoying, and providing a good home for your Akita can be enough. You will find they are among the most loyal and caring pets you can obtain.

Useful Literature and Addresses

Kennel Clubs

Akita Club of America
Dorothy Warren
P.O. Box 2639
Saratoga, CA 95070

American Kennel Club
51 Madison Avenue
New York, NY 10010

For Registration, Records,
  Litter Information:
5580 Centerview Drive
Raleigh, NC 27606

Canadian Kennel Club
111 Eglington Avenue
Toronto 12, Ontario
Canada

The Kennel Club
1-4 Clargis St
Picadilly
London W7Y 8AB
England

Australian National Kennel Council
Boyal Show Grounds
Ascot Vale,
Victoria
Australia

New Zealand Kennel Club
PO Box 523
Wellington 1
New Zealand

Publications

Akita World
4401 Zephyr Street
Wheat Ridge, CO 80033-3299

AKC Gazette
51 Madison Avenue
New York, NY 10010

Dog World
29 North Wacker Drive
Chicago, IL 60606

Books

Bouyet, Barbara. *Akita, Treasure of Japan*, Montecito, CA: M.I.P. Publishing Co., 1992.
Linderman and Funk. *The Complete Akita*, New York: MacMillan Publishing Co., 1983.
Mitchell, Gerald and Kath. *Book of the Breed. The Akita*, Letchworth Herts, England: Ring Press Books, Ltd., 1990.

Index

Activities, 60–65
Age considerations, 26–28
Aggression, 16–17
Agility, 62–63
  trials, 91
American Kennel Club, 11, 14
Anestrus, 71
Appearance, general, 14
Autoimmune diseases, 86–87
Automobile travel, 43

Backpacking, 65
Ball games, 64
Bathing, 58–59
Bloat, 87
Boarding, 54–55
Body, 15
Bonding, 40
Bordetella, 82
Breed:
  AKC acceptance, 11
  characteristics, 12–20
  faults, 70
  history, 10–11, 18–19
  standard:
    Akita Club of America,
      13–14
    American Kennel Club,
      14–16
  stud book, 10
Breeders, 29
  guarantees, 34–35
Breeding, 70–74
  body temperature, 72
  physical examinations, 70–71
  quality, 23–24
  selective, 7
Brood bitch, retirement, 80
Brushing, 58

Calluses, 54
Canine adenovirus, 81

Canine Good Citizen, 61
Canned foods, 68
Carbohydrates, 66
Care, 53–59
  dental, 53–54
  puppy, 75–79
Castration, 57
Children, interactions with, 18
Chondrodysplasia, 23
Coat, 13, 15
  dam's, 79
Coccidia, 83
Collar, 47–48
Color, 13
Colostrum, 76
Combing, 58
"Come" command, 49–50
Commands, 49–52
  clarity, 49
Confinement, 39
Conformation titles, 91–93
Coronavirus, 81–82
Crate training, 46

Dangers, 36–39
Defensive qualities, 17–18
Delivery, 73–74
Dental care, 53–54
Dewclaws, 77
Diarrhea, post whelping, 74
Diestrus, 71
Diet, 66–69
  components, 66
  supplements, 68–69
  weaning, 78
Distemper, 81
Doghouse, 42
Dogsitters, 55
Domestication, 7–8
"Down" command, 51
Dry foods, 68
Dystocias, 74

Ears, 14
  care, 54
Ectropion, 87
Ehrlichiosis, 86
Endoparasites, 83
Entropion, 23, 87
Epilepsy, 23
Estrous cycle, 71
Estrus, 71
Euthanasia, 88–89
Exercise, 60
Eyes, 15
  disorders, 23, 87

Face, 13
Fats, 66
Features, 12–20
Feeding, 41
  frequency, 69
  lactating female, 75
  puppies, 75–76
  trials, 67–68
  See also: Diet, Nutrition
Fences, 43
Fleas, 84–85
Food, 66–68
Forequarters, 15

Gait, 15
Gastric torsion, 87
Gender considerations, 28–29
Glaucoma, 23, 87
Grass awns, 82–83
Grooming, 58–59
Guard dogs, 19

Hazards, 36–39
Head, 13–14
Health:
  care, 80–89
  good, signs of, 32–33
  problems, signs of, 31–32

Heartworms, 83
"Heel" command, 51–52
Hemolytic anemia, 23
Hemorrhage, post whelping, 74
Hepatitis, 81
Herding, 19
Hereditary faults, 22–23
Hide and Seek, 64
Hindquarters, 15
Hip dysplasia, 22–23, 87–88
Homecoming, 36–42
Hookworms, 83
Housebreaking, 46–47
Houseplants, 38
Hunting, 18–19
Hypothyroidism, 23, 86

Intestinal parasites, 83

Kennel, 42

Labor, 73
Leash, 47–49
  training, 48–49
Leptospirosis, 81
Lice, 84
Linebreeding, 23
Lips, 15
Lyme disease, 86

Mammary tumors, 80
Mange, 83
Metritis, 80
Microphthalmia, 23, 87
Mites, 83–84
Muzzle, 14

Nails, 59
Neck, 15
Nesting, 72
Neutering, 55–57
Nose, 14
Nutrition, 66–69
  supplements, 68–69

Obedience:
  titles, 93
  training, 60–61
    importance, 45
Obesity, and spaying, 56–57

Ordate dogs, 10
Ovariohysterectomy See
  Spaying
Ownership considerations,
  25–26

Parainfluenza, 82
Parasites, 83–86
Parvovirus, 81–82
Pedigrees, 90–94
Personality, 16–18, 30–31
Pet:
  quality, 24–25
  shops, 30
  value as, 19–20
Phemphigus foliaceus, 23
Phenotype malleability, 7
Pregnancy, 71–72
Proestrus, 71
Progressive retinal atrophy, 23,
  87
Proteins, 66
Puberty, 71
Puppies:
  care, 75–79
  dental care, 53
  health status, 31–33
  mills, 29–30
  personality, 30–31
  selection, 21, 26–27
  socialization, 78
  teeth, 53
  vaccinations, 78–79
  weaning, 77–78
Puppy proofing, 38–39

Quality:
  breeding, 23–24
  pet, 24–25
  show, 22–23

Rabies, 82
Registration, 35, 90
Ringworm, 83–84
Roadwork, 64–65
Roundworms, 83
Run, 42

Selection, 21–35
Show, 63

quality, 22–23
  standards, 13–14
"Sit" command, 50
Size, 12–13, 15–16
Skijoring, 61–62
Skin parasites, 83–86
Sledding, 19, 61–62
Sniffing games, 64
Socialization, 40
  puppies, 78
Sources, 29–30
Spaying, 55–57, 80
  obesity, 56–57
Species, origins, 6–7
"Stay" command, 50–51

Tags, 48
Tail, 13, 15
Teeth, 15, 53–54
Temperament, 16
  See also: Personality
Temperature, 72, 75
Thrombocytopenia, 23
Ticks, 85–86
Titles, 91
Tongue, 15
Training, 45–52
  crate, 46
  obedience, 45, 60–61
Travel, automobile, 43

Vaccinations, 71, 80–82
  puppies, 78
Veterinarian:
  breeding evaluation, 70
  care, 55
  puppy evaluation, 33–34,
    41
Vogt-Koyanagi-Harada,
  86–87
Vomiting, post whelping, 74

Water, 66
  retrieving, 19
Weaning, 77–78
Weight pulling, 61–62
Whelping, 72–74
Whipworms, 83

Yard, safety issues, 36–37